Alien Identities

Film/Fiction

The Film/Fiction series addresses the developing interface between English and Media studies, in particular the cross-fertilisation of methods and debates applied to analyses of literature, film and popular culture. Not only will this series capitalise upon growing links between departments of English and Media throughout Britain, it also debates the consequences of the blurring of such disciplinary boundaries.

Editors
Deborah Cartmell – I.Q. Hunter – Heidi Kaye – Imelda Whelehan

Advisory Editor
Tim O'Sullivan

Also available

Pulping Fictions: Consuming Culture Across the Literature/Media Divide (1996)

Trash Aesthetics: Popular Culture and its Audience (1997)

Sisterhoods: Across the Literature/Media Divide (1998)

Those interested in proposing contributions to Film/Fiction should contact the editors at the Department of English and the Department of Media and Cultural Production, School of Humanities and Social Sciences, De Montfort University, Leicester, LE1 9BH, UK.

Film/Fiction volume 4

Alien Identities

Exploring Difference in Film and Fiction

Edited by
**Deborah Cartmell, I.Q. Hunter, Heidi Kaye
and Imelda Whelehan**

Pluto Press

LONDON • STERLING, VIRGINIA

First published 1999 by Pluto Press
345 Archway Road, London N6 5AA
and 22883 Quicksilver Drive, Sterling
VA 20166–2012, USA

British Library Cataloguing in Publication Data
A catalogue record for this book is available from the British
Library

ISBN 0 7453 1405 8 hbk

Library of Congress Cataloging in Publication Data
Alien identities: exploring difference in film and fiction/edited
    by Deborah Cartmell ... [et al.].
        p.   cm. — (Film/fiction: v. 4)
    Includes bibliographical references and index.
    ISBN 0–7453–1405–8 (hc.)
    1. Alienation (Social psychology) in motion pictures.
2. Aliens in motion pictures. 3. Monsters in motion pictures.
4. Film adaptations. I. Cartmell, Deborah. II. Series.
PN1995.9.A47A44   1999
791.43'653—dc21   96–46720
                                                          CIP

Designed and produced for Pluto Press by
Chase Production Services, Chadlington, OX7 3LN
Typeset from disk by Stanford DTP Services, Northampton
Printed in the EC by T.J. International, Padstow

Contents

Notes on Contributors

Jonathan Bignell lectures in English and Media at the University of Reading. He is the author of *Media Semiotics: An Introduction,* editor of *Writing and Cinema* and has published numerous essays on aspects of film, television and popular culture.

Deborah Cartmell is Senior Lecturer in English at De Montfort University, Leicester. With Imelda Whelehan, she has recently completed co-editing a book on *Literary Adaptations.* She is presently working on a book on Shakespeare on screen and has written on Spenser, Shakespeare and Afro-American literature.

Martin Flanagan is completing a Ph.D. applying Mikhail Bakhtin's literary theories to film. Recent research has focused on analysing time and space in modern action films using the chronotope, Bakhtin's device for understanding spatio-temporal relations in the text. He teaches film at the University of Sheffield.

Nick Freeman teaches at Bristol University and the University of the West of England and combines work on nineteenth- and twentieth-century English literature with wider interests in post-war popular culture. He has published articles on Swinburne, Mervyn Peake, British film and contemporary fiction, and is currently working on a book about literary responses to late Victorian London.

Liz Hedgecock is currently writing her Ph.D. on authority and masculinity in the male-authored Victorian novel at the University of Salford. Articles are forthcoming on George Gissing and masculinity, the novels of Philip Larkin, imperialism in the Victorian adventure story and *Simpsons* fan websites, and she is currently editing an anthology of Victorian dramatic adaptations.

I.Q. Hunter is Senior Lecturer in Media Studies at De Montfort University, Leicester. He is joint editor of Routledge's Studies in Popular British Film series, for which he has edited *Unearthly Strangers: The British Science Fiction Film*.

Peter Hutchings lectures in Film Studies at the University of Northumbria at Newcastle. He is the author of *Hammer and Beyond* and is currently writing a book on the films of Terence Fisher.

Heidi Kaye is Senior Lecturer in English and Women's Studies at De Montfort University, Leicester, and is particularly interested in popular culture. Forthcoming publications include articles on 'Gothic in Film', *The X Files* and the films *Persuasion* and *Sense and Sensibility* as well as an edition of Elizabeth Gaskell's *Cranford* and other stories.

Patricia Linton is Associate Professor of English at the University of Alaska, Anchorage, where she teaches courses in twentieth-century literature, narrative theory and film. She has published in *Studies in American Indian Literatures* and *Melus* and has articles forthcoming in *Literary Studies East and West* and *Multicultural Detective Fiction: Murder from the 'Other' Side*.

Karin Littau lectures in Film and Literature at the University of Essex. She is interested in the aesthetics and politics of rewriting from both theoretical and material perspectives. She has published articles on film adaptation, translation and rewrites in *MLN*, *Forum for Modern Language Studies* and *Theatre Research International* and is currently completing a book on *Theories of Reading*.

Sharon Monteith is Head of Literature at the University of Hertfordshire and Modern Editor of the literary and cultural studies journal *Critical Survey*. She publishes on American and British fiction and film. She has recently co-edited a book on gender and the civil rights movement and is working on a book on the American South. Two books on Pat Barker are forthcoming.

John Moore is lecturer in Literary Studies at the University of Luton. He has written numerous essays on American culture, science fiction and anarchist writing. He is an Associate Editor of *Anarchist Studies*.

Paul O'Flinn has taught English at Ibibio State College, Nigeria and at Trent University, Ontario. He has also taught sociology at the University of Reading and is currently Chair of the English Studies Department at Oxford Brookes University. Previous publications include *Them and Us in Literature* and *How to Study Romantic Poetry*.

Imelda Whelehan is Principal Lecturer in English and Women's Studies at De Montfort University, Leicester. She is the author of *Modern Feminist Thought* and, with Deborah Cartmell, has recently completed a book on *Literary Adaptations* for Routledge. She is currently writing a book on the impact of anti-feminism in the 1990s.

Introduction – Alien Identities: Exploring Difference in Film and Fiction

Heidi Kaye and I.Q. Hunter

When a gung-ho Will Smith announced in *Independence Day* (Roland Emmerich, 1996) that he couldn't wait to 'whup E.T.'s ass', he cheekily dispelled any lingering affection for our friends from outer space. That Spielberg's amiable alien, a wizened hybrid of Ronald Reagan, a muppet and a foetus, should have been singled out for violent retribution said much about popular culture's hardening attitudes towards 'aliens' of all descriptions. The alien, in every sense of the word, has become central to popular culture. On the one hand, encouraged by programmes like *The X Files*, conspiracy theories proliferate about Roswell, 'grays' and alien abductions. On the other, alien identities of all kinds have been made visible and celebrated by the identity politics which have become central to postmodern culture. We – a problematic word these days – are reminded that otherness and alienation are states of existence not only for imaginary E.T.s but for all who have been excluded from dominant categories of the human, the natural and the native. This volume, the fourth in the Film/Fiction series, ranges widely on the theme of the alien to explore how various cultures and times have determined their own collective and individual sense of identity through external as well as internal contrast. The chapters in the first section consider the alien in the sense of foreigner; those in the second look at humanity's own alien identity; and those in the final part examine ideas of hybridity in the *Alien* film series itself.

The importance of the alien to contemporary culture is reflected in the current wave of American science fiction films. But whereas in the 1970s and 1980s films like *Close Encounters of the Third Kind* (Steven Spielberg, 1977), *E.T.: The Extraterrestrial* (Spielberg, 1982) and *Starman* (John Carpenter, 1984) were modestly optimistic about their strange visitors, 1990s sci-fi has returned with anarchic glee to the 1950s' paranoid injunction to 'keep watching the skies'. It is true that some movies, such as *Contact* (Robert Zemeckis, 1998), still look back sentimentally not only to *E.T.* but to the 1950s' more positive, albeit often highly conservative and patriarchal, representations of the alien: the Christ-like 'Carpenter' of *The Day the Earth Stood Still* (Robert Wise, 1951), for example, and the much abused *Man from Planet X* (Edgar G. Ulmer, 1951).[1] But it is *Alien* (Ridley Scott, 1979) and its sequels which have proved most influential in their fusion of xenocidal horror and misogynistic unease. *Species* (Roger Donaldson, 1995), *Mars Attacks!* (Tim Burton, 1996), *Independence Day* and *Starship Troopers* (Paul Verhoeven, 1997) – like *Alien* – identify the inhuman with monstrous, gloopy, insect-like otherness, and leave no doubt that the only good alien is a dead alien. They offer ironic pastiches of Red-baiting classics such as *The War of the Worlds* (Byron Haskin, 1953), but with a vital political difference: their aliens no longer seem to stand for anything. Instead of metaphors for invading Communists and the dangers of conformism, they are simply and conveniently 'other' – all-purpose outsiders against which the warring chaos of American identities can muster and unite.

To some extent, making aliens the enemy is a politically astute way of avoiding negative representations of identifiable sets of humans. As Paul Verhoeven, the director of *Starship Troopers*, noted: 'The US is desperate for a new enemy ... The communists were the enemy, and the Nazis before them, but now that wonderful enemy everyone can fight has been lost. Alien sci-fi gives us a terrifying enemy that's politically correct. They're bad. They're evil. And they're not even human.'[2] Nowadays only white Englishmen – or Arabs, as in *True Lies* (James Cameron, 1995) – can be safely demonised in action movies. But on closer inspection 1990s sci-fi films, with the ambiguous exceptions of *Starship Troopers* and *Mars Attacks!*, are no less reactionary than their Cold War counterparts. Aliens are irresistibly metaphorical; the films use them to represent alien presences much closer to home. Thus in *Independence Day*, as Michael Rogin and others have suggested, the extraterrestrials are coded as 'gayliens', sexually indeterminate panic objects of the film's homophobia, and are wiped out by a virus.[3] *Men in Black* (Barry Sonnenfeld, 1997) has a cast of intergalactic 'illegal aliens', which suggests fear of invasion from south of the border rather than outer space. And *Species*'s 'alien-babe' is a nightmarish single, white female, whose basic instinct is to kill men and have their babies. In each case the metaphor of the alien taps directly into contemporary anxieties about multiculturalism and gender politics.

The earliest reference to the word 'alien' in the *Oxford English Dictionary* is to its meaning as 'foreign'. The later additional meaning of 'extraterrestrial being' is an obvious extension of this notion of otherness, for the very concept of the alien is grounded in ideas of difference and boundary definitions. It is a commonplace, but still true, that we define ourselves through defining an other: we are what we are not. When our sense of self becomes shaky, we attempt to reconstruct an 'other' from which to distinguish ourselves in a binary opposition. The notion of identity tends to be exclusive rather than inclusive, creating hierarchies and prejudice on the basis of class, race, gender, nationality and sexual orientation. It can be divisive and harmful, defining difference only as negative. What happens if I am not considered one of 'us' but as one of 'them'? Women and minorities know the consequences of this at great cost. However, as some of the chapters in this book demonstrate, reconstructing identities can transform the way a society looks at itself, challenging simplistic boundaries between self and other.

In the end, alien identity is all we have, since we are strangers to ourselves. The strange is made familiar and the familiar strange as we seek to understand ourselves through texts that question our ideas of who we are and what we are not. Whether we look within our society or to other nations, into the future or to another world, we learn about the alien within ourselves which we may not always recognise or want to admit.

In the first chapter of the book, Peter Hutchings sets up two notions of the alien and two political responses to it, which are taken up by the other contributors to the book. The alien, he points out, can be defined as both non-human and foreign, and reactions to it can demonstrate both fear of 'them' and anxiety about 'us'. Hutchings links the first two ideas by the concept of disease as depicted in novels and films about lethal viruses which come from outside national boundaries to threaten the people at home. Whether biological weapons used by foreign powers or pandemics spread by individuals, infectious diseases from Ebola to AIDS tend to be traced back to the Third World, especially to Africa. In the mostly American texts he discusses the virus tends to provoke a military response, if only on the level of metaphor. Yet, Hutchings argues, this reaction is not just xenophobic and racist. These deadly biohazards also signify humanity's fear that nature itself is hostile to us, as if we were a viral parasite to be destroyed by a planetary immune reaction. These nightmare visions of the West's helplessness, despite its technological and military superiority, portray its own self-doubts and its need for reassurance by redefining 'human-ness' in contrast to an alien 'other'.

Sharon Monteith sees a productive contradiction between the definition of alien and citizen, slavery and freedom, property and person. The relationship between Thomas Jefferson and Sally Hemings – master and slave, white man and mulatto woman – has provoked much speculation in fiction, film and history. The incongrous position of black slaves in the newly independent America, in which they were counted as three-fifths human for tax purposes, makes them tautological 'domestic aliens'. Yet Jefferson is an American icon, a 'Founding Father' who wrote the Declaration of Independence which denied 'inalienable' rights to blacks (although he did attempt to outlaw slavery in it, despite being a slave owner). His relationship with Hemings stirs controversy about how questions of race, nationality and citizenship have, from the start, alienated African Americans from the country they helped establish. The largely unknown historical Hemings acts as a metaphor that dramatises the hidden sexual and racial history of the United States. Her story raises issues about the extent to which history is fictionalised and fiction historicised. She offers a place from which to address the black experience that has been unspoken in white America's self-narration of its identity, and a means of confronting not only America's unconscious and conscious racism but also guilt about its slave-owning past.

Britain, with its own imperial past, also defines itself against foreign aliens and racial others. Nick Freeman explores the representation of Britain and the rest of the world in popular spy television series of the 1960s. British television could not afford location filming to provide exotic backdrops for its burgeoning superspy output in the wake of James Bond's success on the big screen. The answer was stock footage of foreign places. These images become iconic through their repetition in programme after programme: Paris is signified by the Eiffel Tower, Rome by the Coliseum and numerous 'banana republics' by palm trees and white suits. 'Swinging London', the cultural capital of this youth-oriented era, represented a revision of national identity in the post-imperial, post-war era. At a time when America, in reality, dominated Britain both politically and culturally, stock images helped Britain comfortably reconstruct the boundaries between nationalities and races and re-establish a sense of stability in a rapidly changing world.

Imperialism and disease haunt *Dracula*, according to Paul O'Flinn's account of Bram Stoker's 1897 novel and Francis Ford Coppola's 1992 film. Stoker's Irish protestant identity and nationalist sympathies placed him in an anomolous position, which is played out in his novel. O'Flinn highlights how Dracula, an alien invader from the East threatening London, the heart of empire, also represents Stoker's own conflicting feelings about supporting and subverting the British Empire.[4] Coppola in turn creates his own mixed messages by associating the vampire with AIDS and its victims. On the one hand, Gary Oldman's Dracula is romanticised and sympathetic. On the other, the film misogynistically represents female sexual desire as ultimately even more dangerous than vampirism. The story's mythic power resides in its ability to absorb the complex, unresolved tensions about identity in various times.

The next few chapters explore the uncanny return of the repressed, as the alien reveals truths about humanity. Time itself is the medium of expressing contemporary fears in both the novel (1895) and film (George Pal, 1960) of H.G. Wells's *The Time Machine*. In visions of the future, the familiar is made alien, yet, as Jonathan Bignell points out, the alien is only comprehensible because it is portrayed via familiar conventions, and the familiar is made strange through changing our manner of perception in both the novel and film. The time travel effect is like cinema itself, speeding up time to show a spectacle, allowing the reader or viewer to become the 'virtual subject' of an experience mediated by text or film. As in the emerging technology of cinema at the end of the nineteenth century, Wells's time machine frees the subject from the real world and its concerns and offers escape through entertainment and commodity consumption.

The breakdown of the distinction between the virtual and the real characterises the computer and filmic effects in Tim Burton's *Mars Attacks!*. As in *The Time Machine*, Wells's novel *The War of the Worlds* and Burton's film show that humanity's greatest threat is itself. Liz Hedgecock argues that Wells and Burton portray human civilisation as degenerate in an evolutionary sense, dominated by technology which turns people into a passive collective; they promote individuality as a sign of 'survival of the fittest'. The aliens are more like than unlike us and are a warning of what we might become.

In Arkady and Boris Strugatsky's *Roadside Picnic* (1972) and Andrey Tarkovsky's *Stalker* (1979) absent aliens leave behind artefacts which promise to fulfil humans' innermost desires and reveal our hidden selves. John Moore analyses the psychological and political resonances of the Soviet novel and film. He sees the journeys in search of extraterrestrial artefacts both as quests into our individual and collective unconscious and as critiques of ideological structures of control which offer the potential for revolutionary change. Such transformation is elusive because of the alienation of everyday life embodied in the outlaw dissident protagonist who attempts to liberate himself from the institutions of the state.

Transformation within and between the various versions of *The Fly* raises issues about narration and re-narration in the short story and films. Karin Littau employs the teleportation machine which produces hybrid monsters as a striking metaphor for the process of adaptation. She examines the breakdown of distinction between original and copy, self and other, human and monster, and explores the repercussions these transgressions entail: loss of authority and alienation.

In the last section of the book, the themes of aliens as foreigners and invaders, of the self as other and of hybridity and mutation come together in discussions of the *Alien* film series. Martin Flanagan takes on the notion of generic hybridity in the various forms which the different films adapt for their own purposes. Gothic horror, war film, dystopia and arthouse cinema combine with big-budget science fiction in an intertextual, inter-species amalgam and Hollywood spawns a brood of monstrous hits.

Finally, Patricia Linton looks back to Mary Shelley's *Frankenstein* (1818) in exploring the relationship between creature and creator in Jean-Pierre Jeunet's film *Alien: Resurrection* (1997) and Kirsten Bakis's novel *Lives of the Monster Dogs* (1997). Despite portraying monstrous fathers and female aliens who signify men's fears of women, these works represent a positive view of female agency which is not linked to their sexual or reproductive nature; instead the bond between women creates its own sustaining power. The novel and film reject the notion of the alien as an absolute other and instead valorise hybridity, suggesting that the survival of the fittest favours the cyborg.

It would seem that the only real alien is the one we carry around inside ourselves. That we humans tend to externalise, categorise and segregate the alien in an attempt to control it shows not only how insecure we are about ourselves, but also how impossible the notion of a single unified self really is. The changing meaning of aliens in contemporary culture, whether they are represented as benevolent or malevolent, reflects very different ideological agenda. We might indeed want to believe – and not only in aliens – but we know that we must trust no one. The contest over defining otherness is clearly a political one. Border crossing, between races, genders, nationalities, even between English and Media, is a political gesture, as the chapters in this volume demonstrate. As in the *Alien* films, the most radically threatening moment is when the alien bursts out of ourselves.

Notes

1. On the politics of 1950s sci-fi, see Mark Jancovich, *Rational Fears: American Horror in the 1950s* (Manchester: Manchester University Press, 1996). On the politics of 1990s sci-fi see I.Q. Hunter, 'From SF to Sci-fi: Paul Verhoeven's *Starship Troopers*' in Jonathan Bignell (ed.) *Writing and Cinema* (London: Longman, forthcoming 1999) and Heidi Kaye, '*Fin de Siècle* Fears: *The X Files* as Contemporary Gothic' in William Hughes, Diane Mason and Andrew Smith (eds), *Legacies of Walpole: The Gothic After Otranto* (Proceedings of the International Gothic Association conference, forthcoming 1999).
2. Rob van Scheers, *Paul Verhoeven*, trans. Aletta Stevens (London: Faber and Faber, 1997), p. xiii.
3. Michael Rogin, *Independence Day, or How I Stopped Worrying and Learned to Love the Enola Gay* (London: BFI, 1998), pp. 54–72. See also Jude Davies and Carol R. Smith, *Gender, Ethnicity and Sexuality in Contemporary American Film* (Edinburgh: Keele University Press), 1998, pp. 149–50.
4. See, for example, Stephen Arata, 'The Occidental Tourist: Dracula and the Anxiety of Reverse Colonization', *Victorian Studies*, (30) 1990, pp. 621–45; Ken Gelder, *Reading the Vampire* (London: Routledge, 1995), Ch. 1; Fred Botting, *Gothic* (London: Routledge, 1996), pp. 144–50.

Further Reading

Barnes, John, *The Beginnings of the Cinema in England* (New York: Barnes and Noble, 1976).

Baxter, John, *Science Fiction in the Cinema, 1895–1970* (London: Tantivy Press, 1970).

Brook, Peter, *Body Work: Objects of Desire in Modern Narrative* (Cambridge, MA: Harvard University Press, 1993).

Clute, John and Peter Nicholls (eds), *The Encyclopedia of Science Fiction*, 2nd edn (New York: St Martins Griffin, 1995).

Davies, Jude and Carol R. Smith, *Gender, Ethnicity and Sexuality in Contemporary American Film* (Edinburgh: Keele University Press).

Haraway, Donna, *Simians, Cyborgs, and Women: The Reinvention of Nature* (New York: Routledge, 1991).

Hardy, Phil (ed.), *The Aurum Film Encyclopedia: Science Fiction*, 3rd edn (London: Aurum Press, 1995).

Huggins, Nathan, *Revelations: American History, American Myths* (New York and Oxford: Oxford University Press, 1995).

Jancovich, Mark, *Horror* (London: Batsford, 1992).

——, *Rational Fears: American Horror in the 1950s* (Manchester: Manchester University Press, 1996).

Jehlen, Myra, *American Incarnation: The Individual, the Nation and the Continent* (Cambridge, MA and London: Harvard University Press, 1986).

Johnson, William (ed.), *Focus on the Science Fiction Film* (Englewood Cliffs, NJ: Prentice-Hall, 1972).

Kuhn, Annette (ed.) *Alien Zone: Cultural Theory and Contemporary Science Fiction Cinema* (London: Verso, 1990).

Landon, Brooks, *The Aesthetics of Ambivalence: Rethinking Science Fiction Film in the Age of Electronic (Re)Production* (Westport, CT: Greenwood Press, 1992).

McGary, Howard, 'Alienation and the African-American Experience' in John P. Pittman (ed.), *African-American Perspectives and Philosophical Traditions* (New York and London: Routledge, 1997).

Morrison, Toni, *Playing in the Dark: Whiteness and the Literary Imagination* (Cambridge, MA and London: Harvard University Press, 1992).

Preston, Richard, *The Hot Zone* (London: Corgi, 1995).

Roberts, Robin, *A New Species: Gender and Science in Science Fiction* (Chicago: University of Illinois Press, 1993).

Rogin, Michael, *Independence Day, or How I Stopped Worrying and Learned to Love the Enola Gay* (London: BFI, 1998).

Schelde, Per, *Androids, Humans and Other Science Fiction Monsters* (New York: New York University Press, 1993).

Shklar, Judith N., *American Citizenship: The Quest for Inclusion* (Cambridge, MA and London: Harvard University Press, 1995).

Slusser, George E. and Eric S. Rabkin (eds), *Aliens: The Anthropology of Science Fiction* (Carbondale, IL: Southern Illinois University Press, 1987).

Sobchack, Vivian Carol, *The Limits of Infinity* (South Brunswick and New York: A.S. Barnes and Co., 1980).

Sollors, Werner, *Neither Black Nor White Yet Both: Thematic Explorations of Interracial Literature* (New York and Oxford: Oxford University Press, 1997).

Sontag, Susan, *Illness as Metaphor/AIDS and its Metaphors* (Harmondsworth: Penguin, 1991).

van Gunsteren, Hessian, 'Four Conceptions of Citizenship' in Bart van Steenbergen (ed.), *The Condition of Citizenship* (London, Thousand Oaks, New Delhi: Sage, 1994).

Wald, Priscilla, *Constituting Americans* (Durham, NC and London: Duke University Press, 1995).

1

Satan Bugs in the Hot Zone: Microbial Pathogens as Alien Invaders

Peter Hutchings

hot (military slang).	Lethally infective in a biological sense.
hot agent.	Extremely lethal virus. Potentially airborne.
hot suite.	A group of Biosafety Level 4 laboratory rooms.
hot zone; hot area; hot side.	Area that contains lethal, infectious organisms.[1]

In March 1998 representatives of several United States federal agencies met to discuss how they would respond to terrorists using biological weapons against American citizens. The imaginary scenario that provided a focus for their discussion involved the release of a deadly virus along the Mexican-American border. At the time it was reported that President Bill Clinton's own concerns about biological warfare had, in part at least, been formed by his reading of books, notably a novel by Richard Preston called *The Cobra Event* (1998) in which a terrorist unleashes a lethal pathogen on New York.[2]

While it is too simplistic to see the March 1998 exercise as issuing directly from a novel or novels, nevertheless it does seem that within the world of hazardous diseases the practices of science, strategic concerns and the telling of scary stories are not readily separable. It is significant in this respect that Richard Preston was best known previously for his factual book *The Hot Zone* which told of the discovery of a strain of the Ebola virus, one of the world's most lethal pathogens, in a monkey house on the outskirts of Washington DC. Preston is not alone in moving between fact and fiction or in his fascination with, to use the jargon, Biosafety Level 4 hot agents. These are fast-acting, highly infectious diseases such as Ebola and Marburg, diseases that in many cases have been known to Western medical science for between twenty and thirty years but which only in the 1990s have acquired a place in the public imagination. Biotech thrillers such as Tom Clancy's *Executive Orders*, Patrick Lynch's *Carriers*, Lincoln Preston's *Mount Dragon* and Pierre Ouellette's *The Third Pandemic*, and films such as Wolfgang Peterson's *Outbreak* (1995) and Terry Gilliam's *Twelve Monkeys* (1995) all offer themselves as being based credibly on scientific understandings of pathogens, while popular science books such as Preston's *The Hot Zone* as well as Laurie Garrett's *The Coming Plague* and Joseph McCormick's and Susan Fisher-Hoch's *The Virus Hunters* will often borrow some of the techniques of fiction in order to dramatise particular scientific concepts and methods.[3] These biologically anxious texts dwell in considerable detail upon the aetiologies of lethal pathogens (both factual and fictional ones) and the protocols of biohazard containment; and in this they contribute towards a broader rewriting of our culture's imaginary terms of engagement with a range of microbial organisms.

Crucial in this process is the figuring of viruses and bacteria as alien, although, perhaps unsurprisingly, this alienness turns out to be a very slippery concept. Indeed, the symbolising of disease seems to go into overdrive here, with alienness – and associated notions of the breaching of borders, of outbreaks and invasions – referring not only to human/non-human difference but also to differences between the West and the Third World and, not least, between different parts of the human body.

This chapter explores the world of the new disease scenarios in terms of alienation. It will argue that what is at stake in the treatment of 'alien' organisms found in these books and films is a species-wide crisis of self-confidence, a crisis that takes the form of a diminution of 'human-ness' in a biosphere increasingly perceived as hostile, so hostile in fact that we need to wear biocontainment spacesuits in order to survive in it. The crisis is predicted in the following terms by Pierre Ouellette in his 1996 biotech thriller *The Third Pandemic*, which tells of a killer bacteria called Agent 57a:

> Humankind had given up on the earth as the center of the solar system some time ago, but it still saw itself at the center of nature, with the biosphere rotating around it in some kind of perpetual servitude. At best, it was seen as some kind of reciprocal arrangement. 'Be nice to Mother Nature, and she'll be nice to you,' as if Homo sapiens had some kind of partial control, and nature would be 'reasonable'. But then along came something like Agent 57a, and suddenly there was no control at all.[4]

A point of reference for a number of the texts discussed in this chapter is Michael Crichton's 1969 novel *The Andromeda Strain*. The Ebola virus in particular is often figured as the real-life equivalent of Crichton's fictional pathogen, so in *The Hot Zone* virologist Karl Johnson is quoted as saying, 'I did figure that if Ebola was the Andromeda strain – incredibly lethal and spread by droplet infection – there wasn't going to be any safe place in the world anyway',[5] while Laurie Garrett's *The Coming Plague* states that 'the Andromeda strain nearly surfaced in Africa in the form of Ebola virus'.[6] Garrett also quotes Karl Johnson, this time in the context of an exercise staged in 1989 by the American Society of Tropical Medicine and Hygiene to test official responses to an Ebola-like epidemic breaking out in Africa: 'You say this might be a mutant strain of Ebola that is respiratorily transmitted. Well, if that is the case, it would be very close to Andromeda.'[7] *The Virus Hunters* comments thus on Ebola: 'It was so cryptic and diabolical that it reminded me of the fictional epidemic from outer space described in The Andromeda Strain.'[8] While containing no reference to Andromeda, Tom Clancy's blockbuster thriller *Executive Orders* describes Ebola in comparable extraterrestrial terms, as 'an alien virus, something almost from another planet'.[9]

Crichton's groundbreaking novel (filmed by Robert Wise in 1970) deals with the scientific response to the discovery of a lethal pathogen brought back from outer space by a satellite. It set the standard for the biotech thriller genre and it is not difficult to see why it still exerts such an influence on later authors. Its description of the decontamination procedures undergone by scientists as they progress through a series of increasingly sterile levels to the laboratory where Andromeda waits for them, as well as the use of spacesuits within the lab, anticipates the practices of biohazard containment that are so important to the 1990s narratives. In addition, the novel's cool, dispassionate prose and its extensive use of scientific terms – the narrative is presented in the form of an official report – are emulated in many later accounts of disease. Andromeda itself functions in *The Hot Zone*, *The Coming Plague* and *The Virus Hunters* as a kind of shorthand, denoting a pathogen that kills just about everything, is highly infectious, fact-acting and incurable, a disease that, in Richard Preston's words, represents 'a species-threatening event'.

It should be pointed out that this use of Andromeda entails an almost wilful misreading of Crichton's novel. Like a number of Crichton's later works, *The Andromeda Strain* is as much concerned with the failure of human systems as it is with the nature of disease. In fact, it can be read as a kind of black comedy where everything that can humanly go wrong does go wrong, to the extent that it is the laboratory's own containment devices, notably a nuclear bomb designed to purge all traces of infection, that threaten the scientists far more than the disease ever did.[10] As for Andromeda itself, it simply mutates into a benign form and floats away into space. Seen in this context, assigning Ebola an Andromeda-status constitutes an attempt to make the virus as scary as possible. Even within the pseudo-scientific terms adopted by these texts, there seems little basis for such a comparison. Andromeda, after all, is a crystalline, self-replicating organism from outer space while Ebola is an earthbound virus that can only replicate within a host cell. Indeed, when one looks back at the passages quoted above, one gains a sense that Ebola does not quite match up to its fictional predecessor: 'Andromeda nearly surfaced' (but it didn't); 'if Ebola was the Andromeda strain' (but it wasn't); 'if that is the case, it would be very close to Andromeda' (but it wasn't the case). Of all the books that invoke Andromeda, only *The Hot Zone* acknowledges that, ultimately, Andromeda is not a species-threatening pathogen. Given that the Washington form of Ebola investigated in *The*

Hot Zone turns out to be lethal only to monkeys and not to humans, it would be difficult for the book to do otherwise. 'It was behaving like the fictional Andromeda strain. Just when we thought the world was coming to an end, the virus slipped away, and we survived.'[11] Even here, however, the comparison with Andromeda is strained, so to speak, for while Andromeda was at least initially lethal, Ebola Reston (as the Washington virus came to be known) appears to have been benign all along. The latter part of *The Hot Zone* works hard to overcome what, in the book's terms, must be something of an anticlimax through figuring Ebola Reston as merely a warning of more dangerous things to come. 'Just at the moment when Nature was closing in on us for a kill, she suddenly turned her face away and smiled. It was a Mona Lisa smile, the meaning of which no-one could figure out.'[12]

In fact the idea of a pathogen – be it a virus or bacteria – that threatens the very existence of humanity probably owes less to *The Andromeda Strain* than it does to a type of fiction best exemplified by Alistair MacLean's 1962 novel *The Satan Bug* (originally published under the pseudonym Ian Stuart). Germ warfare fiction rooted firmly in Cold War tensions, *The Satan Bug* is not especially interested in the operations of science, more in the ways in which pathogens might be used as strategic weapons (although in the novel the true villain turns out to be a Mafioso who wants to provoke an evacuation of London in order that he and his associates can rob a series of banks). Yet the description of the Satan Bug itself is an evocative one. Here is the novel's description of what would happen if a salt spoon full of the Satan Bug was released into the environment:

What happens? Every person in Mordon would be dead within an hour, the whole of Wiltshire would be an open tomb by dawn. In a week, ten days, all life would have ceased to exist in Britain. I mean all life ... Long before the last man died in agony, ships or planes or birds or just the waters of the North Sea would have carried the Satan Bug to Europe. We can conceive of no obstacle that can stop its eventual world-wide spread. Two months I would say, two months at the very most.[13]

Why Satan? It's not to do with the bug itself which, unlike Ebola, remains uncharacterised, but derives instead from the people who would use it – evil people, much like the Iranian villains in *Executive Orders* who launch an Ebola attack on America or the various military figures who seek to control and use lethal pathogens as weapons (see the film *Outbreak* in particular for examples of this). More generally, designating a pathogen as evil places it securely within a recognisable and therefore reassuring context. Even when the disease is a natural rather than a designed pathogen, a sense of evil intent makes it more readily assimilable within a human morality and a human-centred way of seeing the world, to the extent that its assault upon us merely demonstrates how important we still are in the biosphere. If it is the disease with our name on it, then that name has been written by Satan in a language that we can understand. Of course, the recent biotech thrillers are too concerned with their 'scientific' integrity to embrace openly such an unscientific position, although it is present in some of the language they use. Note, for instance, the quotation from *The Virus Hunters* given above which describes Ebola as diabolical or Tom Clancy's comment on Ebola: 'if there were a devil in creation, then this was his gift to the world'.[14] It is also apparent in an almost palpable longing for the species-threatening event, the extinction that perversely would guarantee our species's importance. As Susan Sontag observes in the context of a discussion of HIV and AIDS:

> The taste for worst-case scenarios reflects the need to master fear of what is felt to be uncontrollable. It also expresses an imaginative complicity with disaster. The sense of cultural distress or failure gives rise to the desire for a clean sweep, a tabula rasa. No one wants a plague, of course. But yes, it would be a chance to begin again. And beginning again – that is very modern, very American, too.[15]

With the idea of plague as God's punishment for sin now thoroughly discredited after it was used to stigmatise gays with AIDS, it seems that all we have left to us is Satan, and even this is no longer tenable, a faintly embarrassing holdover from more credulous times.

'People applied all manner of false images to disease. It would lie in wait for its chance; it would kill without mercy; it would seek out victims. All of that was anthropomorphic rubbish, Moudi and his colleagues knew. It didn't think. It didn't do anything overly malevolent.'[16] This passage from Tom Clancy's *Executive Orders* expresses a sense of the resistance of the Ebola virus, and pathogens generally, to metaphor, something that is apparent in all the other books cited here even though at the same time they use metaphors to characterise disease. This quality of the virus, this indifference, might be seen as betraying a distinctly Andromedean quality; it is the indifference of the alien understood in this instance as a kind of alterity, a radical otherness that threatens to tilt the world away from human-centred definitions of it. Judith Williamson's comments on the perception of the HIV virus are relevant here:

> Nothing could be more meaningless than a virus. It has no point, no purpose, no plan; it is part of no scheme, carries no inherent significance. And yet nothing is harder for us to confront than the complete absence of meaning ... for meaninglessness isn't just the opposite of meaning, it is the end of meaning and threatens the fragile structures by which we make sense of the world.[17]

What distinguishes the 1990s disease books and films from the material about which Williamson is writing is the way in which they draw upon various registers of alienness in their attempts to define and protect a particular sort of 'humanness'. On the one hand, hot pathogens are presented as foreign, alien invaders whose activities provoke a military or quasi-military response on the part of the country or person attacked. On the other hand, however, the same pathogens are located in relation to theories of biological evolution which, contrary to Williamson's 'end of meaning', bestow upon viruses and bacteria a very precise meaning in a broader scheme of things. It is a meaning that is scientific enough to merit inclusion, in fact cannot be ignored, but which at the same time opens up a disturbing sense of humanity's position within the biosphere. The tension between these two positions – between what might be termed a Satanic self-confidence and an Andromedean self-doubt – generates many of the ambiguities and contradictions in the 1990s disease scenarios.

A key location in many of the books and films discussed here is Africa which, as elsewhere in Western representation, seems to function more as an imaginary site – the Dark Continent, the cradle of civilisation, the mother of all hot zones – than it does as an area of the world with its own history and cultures. Both *The Hot Zone* and the film *Outbreak* begin in Africa, the former in Kenya in 1980, the latter in Zaire in 1967. In each case, the African landscape is presented as a foreign, alien and potentially dangerous terrain for any whites who dare enter into it. In *The Hot Zone* the man in question is a European, Charles Monet, whose sightseeing tour of a mountain in Kenya is recounted in some detail. Our response to this 'travelogue' is inevitably coloured by the fact that early on Preston informs us that Monet is going to die. With this knowledge in mind, and a growing suspicion (fully encouraged by the book) that the unfortunate Monet is to be infected on this trip, we fearfully scan the landscape looking for potential sources of disease. That the actual source of the pathogen – Marburg virus, in this instance – is never revealed means that the mountain in question, and especially the part of it called Kitum Cave, remains a source of mystery and unspecified danger. When Preston himself makes a journey to Kitum Cave at the end of the book, he, unlike Monet, dresses for the landscape. He wears a biocontainment spacesuit, and Africa becomes another planet.

Spacesuits also feature in the opening sequence of *Outbreak* when two American doctors are flown, suitably besuited, into what appears to be a war zone. In this scene of military conflict a new pathogen – a fictional one called Motaba – has just emerged. At a camp full of dead and dying mercenaries, the doctors extract a blood sample from an American sufferer, then leave, promising to send help. As these 'doctors' are actually American military searching for biological weapons, it is not surprising that when the help does come, it takes the form of a bomb which destroys the camp and everyone in it. One of the most striking things about this sequence is that it does not even try to explain why there should be warfare in Zaire in

1967. Presumably what we see relates to a Zairian civil conflict involving foreign mercenaries that was actually taking place at this time. Not that this matters for the film which, in the interests of defining the African terrain as a strange and alien world, drains it of its history and its politics so all that we have left after the climactic explosion is a pack of monkeys, vectors of the disease, running past the camera.[18] It is worth noting also that of the two American soldiers we see at the beginning, the one who subsequently displays guilt over the bombing is played by African American actor Morgan Freeman. While his race is never ostensibly an issue in the film – and the only time we see him in Africa he is wearing a spacesuit which conceals his racial identity – there is a tacit sense here, if only through Freeman's association with earlier roles which did offer themselves in racial terms (*Glory* (Edward Zwick, 1989), *Driving Miss Daisy* (Bruce Beresford, 1989)), of a character whose blackness is in some way significant. However, an explicit engagement with the position of the African American within American society and history runs the risk of destabilising, or at the least making difficult, the representation of Africa as an alien terrain. It could be argued in this respect that *Outbreak* works to efface racial difference within America precisely in order to preserve the imaginary Africa/America, nature/civilisation dichotomy upon which so much of its alien-centred drama depends.

Both *The Hot Zone* (after detailing Monet's gruesome death and the mini-outbreak this provoked) and *Outbreak* then move to America and a 'normality' defined overwhelmingly in familial terms. In *The Hot Zone* we are introduced to Nancy Jaax as she prepares a meal for her children; it is quickly revealed that both Major Jaax and her husband are veterinary surgeons at USAMRIID (United States Army Medical Research Institute of Infectious Diseases) and are shortly to be involved in the Ebola Washington outbreak. In *Outbreak*, after a short excursion into a hot lab, normality takes the form of another couple, this time recently separated, the man (Dustin Hoffman) based at USAMRIID and the woman (Rene Russo) at the civilian Centres for Disease Control, arguing over the guardianship of the dogs that seem to function as their surrogate children. As the movie progresses, their gradual reconciliation will provide a counterpoint to the spread of the hot Motaba pathogen.

The battle lines are drawn: on the one side there is family and home, on the other foreign pathogens whose furtive entrance into the home country, secreted in the bodies of unwitting carriers, renders them illegal aliens and provokes a militaristic response from the authorities. Hence the centrality of USAMRIID in both *The Hot Zone* and *Outbreak*. Viewed in the cold light of day, this militarisation of the situation does not make much sense; in neither book nor film are the pathogens being used as weapons against America (although, as we have seen, the military in *Outbreak* are interested in acquiring pathogens as weapons). However, on another metaphorical level it makes perfect sense for, as Susan Sontag has pointed out:

> military metaphors have more and more come to infuse all aspects of the description of the medical situation. Disease is seen as an invasion of alien organisms, to which the body responds by its own military operations, such as the mobilizing of immunological 'defences', and medicine is 'aggressive', as in the language of most chemotherapies.[19]

When under attack from outside, what is required is a violent repelling of the invader and the restoration of borders; in a context where homologies proliferate, the military becomes the immune system of the body politic, and the victims of the disease become, in the words of *Outbreak*'s most hawk-like general, 'casualities of war'. As if to justify this militarisation, the pathogens themselves are often defined as weapons, even when they are not being used as such. So in *The Hot Zone* a disease carrier is 'a human virus bomb'[20] and the virus-infected Charles Monet 'had been an Exocet missile that struck the hospital below the water line'.[21] Using similar terminology, the fact-based *The Coming Plague* talks of viruses as having 'payloads and delivery systems'.[22]

Sometimes the activities of these alien invaders assume an insurrectionary tone that might be seen as a caricatural reflection of unstable Third World political regimes. In *The Third Pandemic*, for instance, the emergence of a resistant strain of bacteria is described thus: 'A new political party had emerged, bent on restoring the greatness of the species, dedicated to waging a seemingly suicidal war against the vast armies of immunity.'[23] A comparative sense of rebels overthrowing the state can be found in *The Hot Zone*: 'Your body becomes a city under siege, with its gates thrown open and hostile armies pouring in, making camp in the public squares and setting everything on fire.'[24] As the 'enemy' pathogens take over the bodies of their hosts, these disease narratives also adopt some of the features of the extraterrestrial invasion scenario, with the focus on the secret possession of humans and associated notions of colonisation inevitably bestowing a science fiction tone on the proceedings. The paranoia this produces – who is the alien, who carries the pathogen – again leads us back to the perceived need for a military response, even when there is no ostensible reason for such a response.

Drawing the line in this way, seeking to separate *us* from *them*, our country (usually the United States) from their country (usually somewhere in Africa), can in its clarification of borders be seen as a movement towards reassurance. However, as has already been indicated, another disease discourse is at work in many of these books and films, one which stealthily undermines the confidence implicit in the us/them distinction and which registers a further twist in the concept of alienness. This is perhaps most apparent in some of the ambiguities attached to the very idea of biocontainment. Everyone agrees that a hot disease outbreak needs to be contained: 'There was no vaccine for Ebola ... That left only biocontainment';[25] 'containment is the only option';[26] 'What we want is to nail this virus to the floor and put a big fence round it so nobody else can get hurt'.[27] In order to contain the outbreak, you need to wear a containment spacesuit, yet what is contained in this suit is not the disease but rather the human. That is to say, there is a reversibility implicit in the very idea of containment as it operates here which on certain occasions carries over to the way the pathogens themselves are represented. To put it another way, there is a suspicion in many of the new disease scenarios that biocontainment borders tend to keep *us* in rather than *them* out and that instead of humans defining the pathogen, pathogens and all they represent might be defining the nature of the human. Or, as *The Hot Zone* states, 'The organism was too frightening to handle, even for those who were comfortable and adept in space suits. They did not care to do research on Ebola because they did not want Ebola to do research on them.'[28]

Even as the 1990s disease scenarios stress the foreignness of the pathogen (and, the reverse side of this, the stability of our own identity), they also acknowledge that the pathogen belongs to and is an expression of the natural world. For example, *The Hot Zone* describes Marburg virus as showing 'a kind of obscenity you see only in nature'[29] and comments that Ebola virus particles 'were the face of Nature herself, the obscene goddess revealed naked. This thing was breathtakingly beautiful. As he stared at it, he found himself being pulled out of the human world into a world where moral boundaries blur and finally dissolve completely.'[30] This invoking of nature as an obscene female deity is reminiscent of Judith Williamson's Kristevan-influenced ideas about the way in which the very notion of the virus threatens systems of implicitly patriarchal meaning. In the case of *The Hot Zone*, one of the more militarised texts under discussion here, this registers, arguably, as a kind of hysterical reaction to the closeness of the virus.

Elsewhere – both in *The Hot Zone* itself and other books and films – a more ecological tone is apparent. For example, the emergence of hot pathogens from tropical regions is often seen as arising from Western capitalistic interventions into and destruction of previously stable ecospheres: for example, 'The emergence of AIDS, Ebola, and any number of other rainforest agents appears to be a natural consequence of the ruin of the tropical biosphere.'[31] The agents themselves are readily transmissible not only because of their own innate virulence but also because of their access to modern, worldwide transport systems. 'A hot virus from the rain forest lives within a twenty-four-hour plane flight from every city on earth.'[32] Inasmuch as late Western capitalism depends on an international interconnectedness, and the unrestricted movement of goods and information, the new hot pathogens, to borrow a phrase used by Susan Sontag to describe AIDS, become 'dystopian harbingers of the global village'.[33] In this context, containment becomes a yet more problematic concept, dependent as it is on the closing down of borders and the restriction of movement. This is perhaps most evident in the novel *Executive Orders* where, in the ultimate isolationist act, all of the United States' external and internal borders are sealed off in order to stop an Ebola outbreak spreading. Paradoxically, this action seems to represent a denial of the very national identity that the containment is meant to protect.

Seen in this way, hot pathogens enact the revenge of nature against a Western civilisation which is deeply destructive of that nature. A passage from *The Hot Zone* is revealing here: 'In a sense, the earth is mounting an immune response against the human species. It is beginning to react to the human parasite.'[34] Yet another reversal is apparent, one in which the immune systems, instead of involving our military attacking the pathogens, consists of the pathogens attacking human agents. Are we the alien pathogens now? Certainly one of the characters in *Carriers* seems to think so: '"We should never have come," she said, softer now, as if reading from a book. "We're the disease here. We're the virus. The forest knows that. And it wants to destroy us."'[35]

While the new disease scenarios sometimes represent the excursion of the West into the 'natural' Third World as a kind of alien invasion, they also in certain circumstances figure the body itself as an alien terrain, as alien, in its way, as the African landscape. For example, in *The Hot Zone* a cell viewed through an electron microscope is described as 'an aerial view of rain forest. The cell was a world down there, and somewhere in that jungle hid a virus.'[36] This contemplation of the body as an object in itself, as a thing curiously detached from identity, can be seen as having a distinctly uncanny quality to it. In a classic essay Freud has argued that the uncanny is a class of the frightening which is 'nothing new or alien, but something which is familiar and old-established in the mind and which has become alienated from it only through the process of repression'.[37] What seems to have been repressed in this instance, and is now returning with a vengeance, is a sense of an evolutionary history in which humanity is merely one species among many rather than the fulcrum around which the whole of the biosphere turns. The rain forest inside the cell, the monkey cell in this case, thereby becomes an unwelcome memory of a human bond with a jungle that in its obscene proliferation of species symbolises this history. In this respect the monkeys that carry lethal pathogens from Africa to America in both *The Hot Zone* and *Outbreak* act as a reminder of humanity's own evolutionary origins and our connection with a natural world from which we have ever sought to distance ourselves. This revealing of origins becomes startlingly literal in *Carriers* when it is proposed that a deadly virus was incorporated into the human genetic structure at an early stage in the evolution of the species as part of 'a little neighbourly dispute between two sets of DNA strands that was settled half a billion years ago'.[38] The virus's pathogenic qualities were suppressed by enzymes in order that its replicative abilities could be safely deployed within the human gene sequence. As a consequence of a late twentieth-century genetic experiment this viral structure is liberated. The novel offers the following scenario:

> Florists in Chicago start stocking a new South American cactus, whatever. It flowers once a year. Kid walks by the florist, catches a whiff of cactus pollen. A chemical signal on the pollen surface is recognised. Suddenly the genes coding for the virus light up, and half the population of Chicago dies of a viral haemmorrhagic fever.[39]

Here, in what must be the ultimate return of the repressed, the lethal pathogen, that which is alien to and threatens the existence of the human race, is shown as arising from the very history and substance of humanity itself.

Trapped in our containment suits, with (to use *The Hot Zone*'s evocative phrase) the 'pressure of life' pushing in on us from outside, suddenly we are confronted with the possibility of this pressure coming from within. All the borders erected between us and the biological other are revealed as inadequate; and a sense of humanity as defined via its difference and its specialness, as a species that is in some way apart from the continuum of biological, natural processes, no longer seems viable. Here is another version of the species-threatening event, one which refers to the diminution of the human self-image within the biosphere as our increased scientific knowledge of humanity appears to be writing our own species out of the script. The response of the new disease scenarios to this threat is to re-erect borders, to externalise the threat and mark it as foreign, alien, even as the very scientific concepts used to do this are undermining this project. Another facet of this response is what must register in the scientific or quasi-scientific terms of these texts as an unquantifiable, irrational commitment to human relationships and emotions – hence the re-formation of the couple in *Outbreak* and the Jaax family at the heart of *The Hot Zone*. A gesture of reactionary denial, this commitment also functions within the disease scenario as that most atavistic, non-scientific act – an expression of faith. As the conclusion of *Carriers* puts it:

> She wanted to go back home. More than at any time in her life she needed her family. And they needed her. That was the one truth that had emerged from the whole sordid affair. And if this feeling was partly a genetic thing, something in her chromosomes which made her need her offspring, it was something else too. And whatever it was, it was a human thing, a thing she felt, something that made her more than a living, replicating machine, something more than a virus.[40]

One of the more memorable sequences in *Outbreak* occurs in a cinema during a film screening. A member of the audience, an unwitting carrier of the deadly Motaba virus, coughs and, with the help of special effects technology, we are able to see the tiny droplets of infected water he expels as they float across the auditorium to be inhaled by the next victim of the pathogen. Here, in a very direct way, *Outbreak* puts us, another audience in an auditorium, into the picture. This could be you, it says, you are vulnerable, infectable.

Something similar takes place in the opening section of *The Hot Zone* when an infected Charles Monet is flying to Nairobi on a cramped plane. At a certain point the author abandons the impersonal tone of the preceding pages and addresses the reader as if he or she is actually present on that plane:

> When a man appears to be dying in an airline seat next to you, you may not want to embarrass him by calling attention to his problem ... You say to yourself that this man will be all right. Maybe he doesn't travel well in aeroplanes. He is airsick, the poor man ... Oh God, is he dead?[41]

Again you are placed in close proximity to the infected one, yourself open to infection. There can be no distance here, only an overwhelming sense of closeness.

These moments suggest that the new disease scenario seeks to scare us, and scare us badly. The reasons for this may vary – the factual *Coming Plague*'s concern with public health policies, for example, is not shared by any of the novels discussed in this chapter – but the scare factor is invariably high. The fearful tone this involves carries over into a maximisation of a pathogen's lethality and virulence and an accompanying fetishisation of Biosafety Level 4 procedures. (The novel *Mount Dragon* – partly written by the brother of *The Hot Zone*'s author – even invents a fictitious Level 5 to house genetically engineered viruses that are more deadly than those stored at Level 4.) 'Try to remain calm', ran the slogan used to sell *Outbreak*, functioning in this context as a challenge, one which the film-makers confidently expect the film's audience to fail.

The proliferation of categories of alienness, where at certain moments microbial pathogens, Africa and the human body are all marked as alien, points to a deep-seated anxiety at work here about species identity and the limits of the human. Given widely publicised developments in gene technology and cloning as well as an increasing awareness of the damage wreaked upon the natural world ecology by the actions of capitalism, a response of the kind found in the new disease scenarios is not entirely unexpected. Talking up the pathogen, representing it as an absolute, produces a yield of terror and thereby forecloses on any significant negotiation with issues raised by the pathogen, issues to do with the West's relation to other parts of the world and to the ecosphere generally.

To a certain extent, the proliferation of metaphors around particular diseases is enabled by the fact that (at the time of writing at least) there is no group of Level 4 infectees in the West and there has been no widespread Level 4 Western outbreak in living memory. What this means is that while the Level 4 pathogen is intimidatingly frightening, it also takes on an aura of fantasy, becoming a kind of alien monster liberated from reality's constraints. The same can not be said of the world's most discussed and publicised pathogen, the HIV virus. As both *The Hot Zone* and *Outbreak* inform us, this particular pathogen doesn't even make it into Level 4. Yet it is a disease that is established in the West already, a disease embedded in a range of discourses, many of them articulated by the infected themselves; in short, a weighty disease unlike the excitingly hot Level 4 pathogen. While some of the elements deployed in the new disease scenario have also been used for HIV and perhaps even derive from it – the movement from monkey to human, the movement from Africa to the West – the sort of narrative where carriers become 'virus bombs' or Exocet missiles and where pathogenic death is a gruesome spectacle, and in which the pathogen itself becomes a kind of alien monster, would not generally be thought of now as acceptable in the context of HIV. The victims are too visibly there, their voices too hard to ignore. As Susan Sontag has noted:

> were AIDS only an African disease, however many millions were dying, few outside of Africa would be concerned with it. It would be one of those 'natural' events, like famines, which periodically ravage poor, overpopulated countries and about which people in rich countries feel quite helpless. Because it is a world event – that is, because it affects the West – it is regarded as not just a natural disaster. It is filled with historical meaning.[42]

Ebola and its companion Level 4 pathogens lack the sort of historical meaning discussed by Sontag and because of this they offer opportunities for the entertaining and to a certain extent exorcising of fears and anxieties. In this respect, fighting the new diseases is a bit like Rambo refighting Vietnam; after the initial historical trauma that is AIDS or Vietnam, an imaginary victory can finally be secured.

But such fantasies always come at a cost. In particular, the identification of other cultures and other countries as alien involves a kind of cultural solipsism, a refusal to engage with notions of otherness as anything other than as a threat to the integrity of the (implicitly white) Western self. While it is tempting to assign the morbid scenes of self-destruction apparent in these works to a kind of pre-millennial gloom, such a reading misses out on the way in which the disease scenarios operate as fantasies of powerlessness issued from a position of power, from a Western perspective characterised by highly advanced biotechnologies, immensely powerful military systems and significant material wealth. That there is on certain levels a recognition of this in most of the books and films discussed here is a hopeful sign. It is as if the very material from which they have been fashioned resists the easy erection of borders and designation of alien zones. One looks forward to a time when pathogens are simply pathogens and nothing more, and the interconnectedness of the global ecosystem becomes a focus for identity rather than a threat to it. Such a change would require from the West a greater sense of its own relativeness. If nothing else, the new disease scenarios have put a dramatisation of such relativity into play within popular discourse, if only ultimately to close it down.

As things stand at present, we seem to be stuck with a response to virulent disease which, for all its sophisticated technological knowledge, does not appear to have advanced far, in coming to terms with otherness at least, from Daniel Defoe's advice from 1722: 'the best physic against the plague is to run away from it'.[43]

Satan Bugs in the Hot Zone? Try to remain calm.

Notes

1. Richard Preston, *The Hot Zone* (London: Corgi, 1995), pp. 373–4.
2. 'War Games Show Up Germ Defences', *Guardian*, 28 April 1998.

3. Tom Clancy, *Executive Orders* (London: Harper Collins, 1998); Laurie Garrett, *The Coming Plague* (Harmondsworth: Penguin, 1995); Patrick Lynch, *Carriers* (London: Mandarin, 1996); Joseph McCormick and Susan Fisher-Hoch, *The Virus Hunters* (London: Bloomsbury, 1996); Pierre Ouellette, *The Third Pandemic* (London: Hodder, 1997); Lincoln Preston, *Mount Dragon* (London: Bantam, 1997).
4. Ouellette, *The Third Pandemic*, pp. 325–6.
5. Preston, *The Hot Zone*, p. 129.
6. Garrett, *The Coming Plague*, p. 6.
7. Ibid., p. 594.
8. McCormick and Fisher-Hoch, *The Virus Hunters*, p. 134.
9. Clancy, *Executive Orders*, p. 208.
10. See Mark Jancovich, *Horror* (London: Batsford, 1992), pp. 92–3.
11. Preston, *The Hot Zone*, p. 322.
12. Ibid., p. 322.
13. Alistair MacLean, *The Satan Bug*: this novel has been reprinted numerous times in various editions. The description of the Satan Bug occurs in Chapter 3.
14. Clancy, *Executive Orders*, p. 277.
15. Susan Sontag, *Illness as Metaphor/AIDS and its Metaphors* (Harmondsworth: Penguin, 1991), p. 173.
16. Clancy, *Executive Orders*, pp. 456–7.
17. Judith Williamson, 'Every Virus Tells a Story' in Erica Carter and Simon Watney (eds), *Taking Liberties: AIDS and Cultural Politics* (London: Serpent's Tail, 1989), p. 69.
18. The jungle, the helicopter used to transport the medics, the napalm-like bomb are all reminiscent of Vietnam, another 'alien' world where America felt out of place.
19. Sontag, *Illness as Metaphor*, p. 95.
20. Preston, *The Hot Zone*, p. 49.
21. Ibid., p. 69.
22. Garrett, *The Coming Plague*, p. 432.
23. Ouellette, *The Third Pandemic*, p. 45.
24. Preston, *The Hot Zone*, p. 86.
25. Ibid., p. 213.
26. Clancy, *Executive Orders*, p. 988.
27. Lynch, *Carriers*, p. 341.

28. Preston, *The Hot Zone*, p. 84.
29. Ibid., p. 143.
30. Ibid., p. 190.
31. Ibid., p. 365.
32. Ibid., p. 45.
33. Sontag, *Illness as Metaphor*, p. 178.
34. Preston, *The Hot Zone*, p. 366.
35. Lynch, *Carriers*, p. 404.
36. Preston, *The Hot Zone*, p. 188.
37. Sigmund Freud, 'The Uncanny' in *The Penguin Freud Library: Volume 14* (Harmondsworth: Penguin, 1990), pp. 363–4.
38. Lynch, *Carriers*, p. 381.
39. Ibid., p. 382.
40. Ibid., p. 479.
41. Preston, *The Hot Zone*, pp. 48–9.
42. Sontag, *Illness as Metaphor*, p. 169.
43. Daniel Defoe, *Journal of the Plague Year* (London: Dent, 1969), p. 223.

2

America's Domestic Aliens: African Americans and the Issue of Citizenship in the Jefferson/Hemings Story in Fiction and Film

Sharon Monteith

> What, to the American slave, is your Fourth of July? ... this Fourth of July is yours not mine; you may rejoice, I must mourn ... I am not included within the pale of this glorious anniversary![1]

> We, domestic aliens, are its very incunabula – the black, black soul of the United States.[2]

> Independence is not a toy for a child to play with.[3]

America's African Americans are the descendants of slaves, an imported population for whom Thomas Jefferson's Declaration of Independence was the succinct summary of their alien status. Denied the 'inalienable rights' of 'life, liberty and the pursuit of happiness', blacks were denied citizenship on the basis of racial identity and in the Constitution of 1787 counted as three-fifths human for the purposes of calculating property taxes. Eighteenth-century discussions of racial identity and of citizenship as racially determined are represented by Jefferson himself in algebraic notation in his pseudo-scientific castigation of the humanity of those who could be categorised according to the 'one-drop law'.[4] One such mulatto who would have been categorised as three-fifths human, and '$a/2+ A/2$' according to Jefferson's calculations, was Sally Hemings, the woman who is purported to have fathered seven of his

31

children – five of whom survived – and who lived out her life as a slave on his Virginia plantation, Monticello. Hemings became Jefferson's property in 1772 when he inherited her as one of 132 slaves on his marriage to Martha Wayles, Sally's white half-sister, who died ten years later. She remained a domestic alien, ineligible for any of the civic reforms Jefferson championed, throughout the thirty-eight years she was reputedly linked romantically with the third President of the United States.

Sally Hemings never wrote or told her story; little evidence exists to verify her place next to Jefferson and what does exist relies most heavily on her son Madison Hemings's statement in 1873 to an Ohio newspaper in which he attested that he was Jefferson's son. Sally Hemings has remained an enigma and is remembered primarily as the cause of the controversy that almost prevented Jefferson's election for a second term of office in 1804. The journalist James Thomson Callender's infamous poem, 'Dusky Sally', published in 1802 along with his castigation of Jefferson in the *Richmond Recorder*, made Hemings one of the most renowned figures in America for a while but few ever saw her and Jefferson never commented publicly on the scandal. If Hemings was the most talked about woman in America for a time, she was not an American; she was not freed until after her master's death. Jefferson's politics were the politics of the Enlightenment as *Notes on the State of Virginia* (1786) so clearly demonstrates and that a libertarian should pursue a relationship with one of his own slaves strikes at the heart of the American dilemma of race relations. Sally Hemings supposedly looked white, like the mulatta figure who finds herself the protagonist of so many early African American fictions, and her daughter Harriet reputedly passed for white in the North after she turned twenty-one, as others of her family had done if they chose to exist on the white side of the colour-line, once freed or allowed to 'walk' by their father. The interracial American family and the taboo of miscegenation combine in the story of Jefferson and Hemings. Miscegenation was declared illegal in Virginia in 1662 and remained so long after the deaths of Jefferson and Hemings. Their relationship reputedly began in the Hotel Langeac when Jefferson was American Minister to France during the French

Revolution; it was possible because Hemings, then only fifteen years old, was charged with accompanying her master's youngest living daughter on the voyage to Europe in order to deliver the daughter to her father in Paris. Hemings became Jefferson's maid servant on arrival.

In 1974 Fawn Brodie wrote *Thomas Jefferson: An Intimate History* in which she posited Sally Hemings as the love of Jefferson's life and the love story as containing the elements of a national tragedy. If Brodie is believed, at around the age of forty-five Jefferson began a romantic relationship with Hemings despite his public office. We know remarkably little about Hemings the woman, even allowing for Callender's scandalmongering, Jefferson's white descendants' refutations of Callender's claims and Brodie's researches.[5] Is Hemings liberated, revealed or commodified in the fictions or films about her or might each of these factors be operating simultaneously in constructions that ease her out of Monticello and into literary and cinematic representation? It is clear that Sally Hemings is an audacious and controversial figure as deployed across a range of cultural productions, not least when her presence serves to point up the glaring contradictions that made this 'First Lady' an alien in America – a non-citizen in the Republic.

I view the controversial relationship between America's architect of democracy and his slave Sally Hemings as an allegory of the racial drama that made whites 'Americans' and blacks 'aliens'. For Hannah Arendt, slavery is the 'primordial crime' on which 'the fabric of American society [has] rested' and slaves were 'wholly overlooked' in the construction of American nationhood.[6] The historical veracity of their relationship is of less interest to me than the ways in which this legendary, almost mythical, cross-racial and archetypally *American* relationship ghosts the present. It has been continually recast and re-envisioned in fiction and film across two centuries, by whites as well as blacks, in Europe as well as America. William Wells Brown's *Clotel or The President's Daughter* (1853), the first novel to be published by an African American, calls for a moral revolution on the basis of such a relationship. For Brown the mother and father of America are black and white: 'Behold the Mayflower anchored at Plymouth

Rock, the slave ship in James River. Each a parent ...'[7] The image of America is inextricably entangled with the perceived significance of this particular interracial relationship and cross-racial family. Brown is not interested in historical veracity, he plays fast and loose with dates, documentation and details and combines his image of Jefferson with a slaveholder called Carter who sold his slave mistress. However, in *Clotel* the moral authority of the Declaration of Independence which forms its epigraph is scrutinised, together with the Bill of Rights that was intended to promote an egalitarian society. Nothing is permitted to dilute the primary fact that concerns Brown: blacks were domestic aliens whose limited rights could be violated at every turn. Blackness encodes their alien status as surely as the 1662 Virginia law of *partus sequitir ventrum* ensured that children whose fathers were white were accorded the status of the mother, so that a black mother gave birth to slave children. In *Clotel*, the President's daughters are sold: 'two daughters of Thomas Jefferson, the writer of the Declaration of Independence and one of the presidents of the great republic, were disposed of to the highest bidder'.[8] Clotel finally commits suicide within a short distance of the President's home in Washington rather than be returned to slavery. For Brown it is the paradox of American culture that stands at the heart of this novel – the violation of the highest principles of Jeffersonian democracy.

However, it is through Barbara Chase-Riboud's 'Sally Hemings Chronicles', notably *Sally Hemings* (1979), that the story of an interracial drama of human rights has become best known.[9] Chase-Riboud, an African American based in France, had been influenced by Fawn Brodie's book in which the story of Jefferson's alleged relationship with Hemings received its first detailed and most controversial historical treatment and she dedicates the first novel to Brodie. Conversely, Annette Gordon-Reed acknowledges the novels about the relationship as the source and spur to her research for *Thomas Jefferson and Sally Hemings: An American Controversy*. She cites historical novels as 'probably ... the single greatest influence shaping the public's attitude about the Jefferson–Hemings story'.[10] Certainly, fiction provides the space in which to exploit the melodrama of a white public official's unofficial and publically unacceptable intimate relationship with a domestic alien. However, it is the interrelationship of history and fiction that is in many ways the key to continued interest in the controversy since it hits at the heart of the debate about how fictionalised history inevitably is and how historicised fiction can be. Hayden White and Alun Munslow, for example, have argued that historians write figuratively across recognisably literary genres in order to imagine history. Writers of fiction, especially writers of Southern fiction, Ralph Ellison has argued, try 'to tell that part of human truth which we could not accept or face up to in much historical writing because of social, racial and political considerations'.[11] The texts I discuss renegotiate ideas of history and memory as constitutive of America's national past as contrived and constructed to alienate African African contributions. They do so by foregrounding two historical figures who can never be fully known but who for this very reason persist in the literary imagination.

Chase-Riboud has said, 'When I wrote *Sally Hemings* what struck me were the very complicated and convoluted relationships between these two families – the "black" Hemingses and the "white" Jeffersons. That's typically American.'[12] The intimacy with which blacks and whites have lived together, especially in the American South, continues to dominate historical and literary discussions of the Old South, of segregation, and of race relations in contemporary America. It provides the dramatic impetus behind the Merchant/Ivory film *Jefferson in Paris* (1995) which was the controversial subject of more than 400 newspaper articles on its American release.[13] Perhaps the commotion was so marked because in 1979 CBS dropped their option to produce a television drama of Chase-Riboud's *Sally Hemings*, when a small but vocal group of Jefferson scholars balked at the idea of a popular cultural representation based on 'a scandalous rumor'.[14] Subsequent American options have also been dropped and the European film production simply underlines the fact that this love story works as an allegory of America that shows how intimately democracy and political equality have been intertwined with slavery and citizenship. As James Baldwin asserted, slavery remains 'that shadow which lies athwart our national life' and 'the past will remain horrible for exactly as long as we refuse to address it honestly'.[15]

What is to be noted is the number of historians who smarted on the publication of a fiction or the release of a film which encodes images of Jefferson. As pointed out recently, Jefferson has always enjoyed a 'Teflon-coated reputation with the general public'.[16] Reputedly, John F. Kennedy once described a group of Nobel Prize winners as a the most wonderful array of talent to be gathered in a single place, 'with the possible exception of when Thomas Jefferson dined alone'. Jefferson was a polymath, an icon, who has stood for American morals and American character over the centuries, even when, as Wyndham Lewis astutely commented, his legacy has proved to be 'a legacy of unreality, like the dream of a golden age ... It serves to deepen the nonsense supervening, when tough politics and cut-throat business masquerade beneath the homespun of the simple farmer' and 'that delectable Rousseauist democracy, of Jefferson's imagination'.[17] Ishmail Merchant and James Ivory's historical drama actually ensures that Thomas Jefferson is read as a quiet intellectual statesman and a lonely widower whose emotions are awakened by the charm of a young girl who in Paris reminds him of home, of America and most tellingly of Monticello. In fact, rather than enforcing the *droit de seigneur*, Nick Nolte's Jefferson succumbs to a bright young Sally, played by Thandie Newton, after an incredibly literate (historically, the relationship was primarily epistolary) but quite formal flirtation with married Maria Cosway, played by Greta Scacchi. The film is a sumptuous romantic drama set in Louis XVI's court and the Hotel Langeac as one has come to expect from the Merchant/Ivory partnership but it was still variously maligned as a controversial representation of Jefferson's concubine by whom he sired children.[18] Maria Cosway had been an important foil to the Hemings story; historians could cite Jefferson's broken romantic involvement with her as the reason he never married again, arguing that he carried a torch for her until his death. In this film, although Cosway is central to the representation of the Paris years, she is clearly usurped in Jefferson's affections by the young slave.

What the film draws out is how crucial the differentiation between public and private life is to any understanding of how slaves could be described as 'family members' and could become the closest intimates of whites, yet were denied the stability on which ideals of American family life depended. The opening credit sequence shows Jefferson writing to his daughter Martha; the letter he pens is simultaneously copied by a copying machine of his own invention as he writes.[19] Behind the symmetry, however, is asymmetry and the motif of doubling that dominates the *mise-en-scène* bespeaks the existence of two families co-existing in his life – one white and one black, one kin and the other alien, one the public face of a family man whose most private letters were published, the other hidden and shameful. Behind the Merchant/Ivory veneer mysteries lurk. Editing is the structuring principle of *Jefferson in Paris* and points up the contradictions in an effort to systematise the relationships; Jefferson's time in Paris is framed by Madison Hemings's account of his father as told to the reporter from the *Pike County Republican*. The film is not the vertiginous text Steve Erickson's *Arc D'X* (1993) becomes but even its Merchant/Ivory glossing of events refuses to sanitise or erase the anomalies exposed through Ruth Prawer Jhabvala's screenplay.

Like Nathan Huggins, I believe that the relationship that fascinates some writers and repels some historians is '*symbolically* true' in that 'the Sally Hemings story ties a people [African Americans] to the founding of the nation ...'[20] Race has always been a determinant of nationality and citizenship in the United States and, as Myra Jehlen has argued, sex too is a determining factor which 'might be seen as paralleling the "discovery" of America'.[21] Focusing on interracial foundational relationships such as that between Captain John Smith – the white Jamestown colonist – and Pocahontas, as well as the particular relationship under discussion here, helps us to reassess the ways in which sex and race have been submerged within the civic discourse of American national identity. America's interracial history cannot be unlocked, according to Baldwin, 'until we accept how very much it contains of the force and anguish and terror of love'.[22] The women remain alien presences, even the Native American Pocahontas. They have been annexed away from the abstract ideals inscribed in two monumental heroes – Smith and Jefferson – who are axiomatic to the 'invention' of America. Most specifically, Sally Hemings if read in Lyotard's terms is a disavowed *petit récit* in the grand narrative of Jeffersonian democracy.

Writers and film-makers circulate her story around texts and contexts. The Sally Hemings they create is a textual construct who 'lives' through and on the page – or on the screen – whose presence is regenerated as a historical source. She is situated in a discourse of freedom that her presence helps to articulate. In Steve Erickson's *Arc D'X* she eclipses Jefferson when she becomes the white writer's extended metaphor for all the theoretical and moral meanings he seeks to encode in his novel: 'the ultimate insurrectionist had liberated herself of the world's greatest revolutionary'.[23] Fredrick Jameson has discussed what he terms the 'sedimented layers of previous interpretations'[24] when one reads and re-reads down a literary line and, as Sally Hemings is re-read and re-interpreted, her silence – present as she was at the dawning of American Independence – is given voice and her alienation transformed into insurrection by popular fictions like Erickson's post-modernist *Arc D'X*. The kind of fictions and histories which allow Sally Hemings a place or space within them seek to legitimise an illegitimate legacy that has stood outside America's narration of itself.

The problem that Annette Gordon-Reed addresses in her book is that the relationship between a president and his slave has been repudiated and denied without recourse to the evidence, as if to explore would be to expose Jefferson and to leave him vulnerable. It would be difficult and unhelpful to seek to overshadow Jefferson's major contribution to the nation. In any case, it would be impossible. However, to fail to address the relationship's challenge to established public history is to fail because, as another critic has it, 'Slavery pervades nationalism as an ever-present reminder of a political sin, a repressed context always threatening to return and unsettle the foundations of a monumental American culture.'[25] Where writers of fiction and makers of film focus on refiguring that repressed or submerged attachment, it has been left to a small minority of historians to assess the evidence that

Madison Hemings and his mother left as their legacies. Exactly how one embarks on a search for Hemings depends on one's ideological perspective. In the starkest terms, Sally Hemings can be read as representative of the black resource on which white republicanism depended for its economic and national viability but none of the fictions, with the possible exception of *Arc D'X*, even begin to discredit Thomas Jefferson or his significance as a Founding Father in national history. They do not demonise him, for example, in the way of Conor Cruise O'Brien's relentlessly counter-revolutionary *The Long Affair: Thomas Jefferson and the French Revolution 1785–1800* (1996). Rather, the fictions persist in their challenge as to the ways in which he is remembered. They perceive him as trapped by the very same national myths that maintain his legendary status. William Wells Brown is perhaps the most serious challenger, deploying his own first-hand experience of slavery and the paradox of democracy to interpret a very different legacy of Independence from that which has characterised most historical depictions.[26] For Brown, the Declaration is a covenant based on exclusion and oppression. Jefferson was never a particularly active abolitionist but the section of the Declaration that he wrote, which would have outlawed slavery had it been ratified by Congress, remains the anomaly that underpins any interrogation of his possible relationship with Hemings. This was his only concerted attempt to incorporate blacks into the national body and it was strategic since the introduction into America of slavery as an institution was one of the many charges he laid at the door of King George III and the English colonists. For Steve Erickson, Jefferson is caught in a political stranglehold; he is caught between his alleged pursuit of human rights and his pursuit of personal happiness in the form of a beautiful black slave, his very own domestic alien.

Known as 'The Apostle of Americanism', the revolutionary statesman of the free republic continues to figure strongly in contemporary discussions of democracy and America's will to define its identity over the last two hundred years. African Americans were strategically alienated from a political and national discourse of citizenship. Black slaves and free men and women were viewed neither as rational human beings nor as fit for citizenship, unlike immigrants who might forge a relationship with America and subsequently claim it as their own, once confirmed as subjects. Judith N. Shklar opens her study of American citizenship with the statement that 'From the first the most radical claims for freedom and political equality were played out in counterpoint to chattel slavery, the most extreme form of servitude, the consequences of which still haunt us.'[27] Those consequences are played out in novels as different as Hawthorne's *The Marble Faun* (1860) through Miriam who with 'one burning drop of African blood in her veins' is a vulnerable 'American' and Charles Chesnutt's *The House Behind the Cedars* (1900) in which John Walden discovers he is black in North Carolina but white in South Carolina, his alien status revised according to state laws. In Erickson's novel Sally is admonished by her eight-year-old mistress, Polly Jefferson, 'You're a slave and I'm a Virginian' and throughout the text Sally is unable to fully formulate the word 'America' or to utter the word 'Freedom'.[28]

Literary representations of Thomas Jefferson have, since James Callender's assault on the private life of a President, quite regularly encoded the special relationship he is purported to have had with his wife's half-sister as a means of interrogating issues of race and rights. In Ralph Ellison's *Invisible Man* (1952) a character claims to be Jefferson's grandson 'on the "field-nigger" side', while a century earlier in *Uncle Tom's Cabin* (1851–52) Harriet Beecher Stowe had a character assert that 'All men are born free and equal' is 'one of Tom Jefferson's pieces of French sentiment and humbug'.[29] In *The President's Daughter* (1994), her sequel to *Sally Hemings*, Chase-Riboud has Harriet Hemings read Brown's *Clotel* in its original edition: 'I sat reading my "biography" with an eerie feeling of jubilation ... What else could I wish for?'[30] The possibilities abound for writers who choose to distinguish between official history and historiography, what Sally in Chase-Riboud's *Sally Hemings* calls 'my real history' – that peculiarly African American subject position which her daughter Harriet, in *The President's Daughter*, describes in the following way: 'We, domestic aliens, are its very incunabula – the black, black soul of the United States.'[31]

History itself has provided many of the coincidences – or arcs of time to use Erickson's metaphor – so appealing to writers of fiction. Just as Thomas Jefferson and John Adams came together with Congress to ratify the Declaration of Independence on 4 July 1776, so they died on the same day in 1826 as fireworks and parades celebrated the fiftieth anniversary of its signing. The then President, John Quincy Adams, declared this a 'strange and very striking coincidence'.[32] The date has particularly ironic significance too for the descendants of slaves when one remembers that Sojourner Truth, the famous anti-slavery campaigner whose 'Ain't I a Woman' speech has been reprised in verse and in song, was promised her freedom on the day of Jefferson's death but that freedom failed to materialise.[33] Similarly, many of Jefferson's own slaves were auctioned on his death to relieve some of the considerable debt on his estate. Slaves were entirely cognisant of the symbolic import of 4 July for all those unlike themselves whose sense of liberty was redoubled on that day. Denmark Vesey and Nat Turner each staged their slave rebellions on that date in 1822 and 1831. Barbara Chase-Riboud acknowledges their dramatic impact when she has her reclusive elderly Sally Hemings attend Turner's trial; she and her son Eston are black witnesses standing unnoticed for the whiteness of their skins in an all-white crowd. In Nat Turner, Chase-Riboud's Sally sees all the ironies of her own hidden history; his public black defiance and insurrection speak to the woman who is hidden from history as she hides her white face in the crowd.[34] It is Sally in this novel who persuades Jefferson to exile the last of Gabriel Prosser's rebels in 1800 rather than hang them. Sally Hemings is attributed with historical agency and can be a solver of moral problems; she is granted an aesthetic freedom that speaks directly to the limitations of American democracy and its avoidance of moral responsibility in creating racial aliens instead of citizens of the republic. Chase-Riboud deploys her researches to full effect; wherever Sally could have intervened in history she does, where she cannot, she provides an alternative in which history becomes an allegory of desire, to 'kill him with love ... And if I could not kill him, I would maim him forever, cripple and paralyze him, so that he would have no possibility to walk away from me, no voice to deny me'.[35] Sally Hemings's exclusion from the grand narrative of America is reconfigured as subversion and desire and is inextricably interwoven with power – legal and national.

Personhood and citizenship have always been constituted by law as contingent, as Martin Luther King, Jr knew only too well and reiterated throughout his speeches.[36] African Americans have historically been excluded from the rights enumerated in the Declaration and made manifest in the Constitution. The Dred Scott decision of 1857 made manifest their particularised exclusion and the *Brown* v. *Board* decision that desegregated public schools was described by one opponent as signalling an imminent 'alien invasion'.[37] Legal exclusion was not reconstituted as citizenship until the 1965 Voting Act. As Priscilla Wald points out in *Constituting Americans*, citizens could not be property and slaves could not be citizens and it is this tautology which upheld slavery[38] – or in Lincoln's words: 'This nation cannot survive half slave and half free.' The film *Amistad* (Steven Spielberg, 1998) turns on this very principle since it is contract law and the distinction between persons and property that form the basis of the trial of the mutinous Africans deemed slaves in America. In fact, slavery is the opposite of citizenship: the totalitarianism of chattel slavery is what elevated the civil rights and liberties of free whites and led them to guard those rights so well. Toni Morrison describes the contradistinction another way. In *Playing in the Dark,* she sees the 'Africanist presence' as carefully positioned as white America's metaphor for all that is 'not-American': 'Africanism is the vehicle by which the American self knows itself as not enslaved, but free; not repulsive, but desirable; not helpless, but licensed and powerful; not history-less, but historical; not damned, but innocent ...'[39] The purposeful alienation of African Americans within the national body is clear whether read according to Marxist theories of alienation or individualist liberal ideas. As Howard McGary argues in 'Alienation and the African-American Experience', however, both theories fail to address the ways in which community can militate against alienation to some degree.[40] Blacks – enslaved or free – were prevented from participating in American society in any sphere other than labour and production but they were not successfully impeded from forging communities. To be American and to be black became mutually exclusive conditions that it took the civil rights movement of the 1960s to break open and examine in law. But, as the texts such as those which focus on the Jefferson–Hemings controversy indicate, blacks as a revolutionary and self-willed presence expose the false principles on which their subjection was justified at the very moment when liberty became the key to citizenship.[41]

Whereas Ruth Prawer Jhabvala and Barbara Chase-Riboud recreate the political and social milieu in which the Jefferson–Hemings liaison would have taken place, Steve Erickson spins much further away from the historical genre and plunges his characters outside history. Steve Erickson propels his Jefferson and Hemings forwards to the year 2000 via labyrinthine historical twists and imaginative turns. He makes the most of his Sally's ex-centric subject position so that Sally Hemings is exigent, she is at once the subject of the novel and the ethical and political field beyond its frame. Erickson asks the kind of question that Ellison's Invisible Man asks: 'What if history was a gambler ... What if history was not a reasonable citizen but a madman ...?' and Erickson's arc functions in the way that Ellison's 'boomerang of history' described curves which spiral down the centuries disfiguring America in national and international terms.[42] In *Arc D'X* history is a tragic conundrum that is offered as an explanation for a degenerative and apocalyptic present and Sally Hemings's personal crisis is represented as a specific curse forged within the crucible of slavery. Hemings becomes a protean figure, whose meaning is much more than the sum of her parts; in Erickson's thesis when Hemings returned to Monticello and slavery instead of remaining in revolutionary Paris as a free woman, she alienated herself from liberty and citizenship at the very moment when in French society the term *citoyen* was coined. Erickson pursues his thesis in a number of directions towards the end of what has often been called 'the American century' and the collapse of history. In one narrative permutation, Hemings escapes Jefferson in Paris. In another, the limited facts intervene and she returns to Monticello. In an ironic twist a character steals the 'Unexpurgated Volumes of Conscious History' that have been hidden by the priestly demagogues of a dystopian city and will return them – re-writing as he does so – only if Sally Hemings is allowed her freedom. In another disorienting incarnation, Jefferson is commanding a slave army while in chains having sold himself to his former slaves as a grotesque figurehead. His death comes not with the fiftieth anniversary of Independence but at the hand of a neo-Nazi on the eve of the new millennium whose pursuit of happiness has led him to an old, dishevelled man lost in time and plagued by memories. Erickson dismantles the dream of America that rests on Thomas Jefferson but elides Sally Hemings. *Arc D'X* interrogates the 'cult of fact' in the most dynamic of ways, incorporating the facts of the relationship as far as they are known, it pushes ahead to supersede them, denying history the last word.

Historically contingent, Sally Hemings is nothing if she is not read as a key figure in exposing the history of racial and sexual relations in the United States. She was a domestic alien in more ways than one; heterotopically in Foucault's sense the space she occupies is delimited as it was for all blacks prior to 1863 and Lincoln's Emancipation Proclamation, and continued to be prior to legislation in the civil rights era. Symbolically, she is slavery personified in all its contradictions and irresolution. When Henry Louis Gates introduces the Schomberg collection of women's slave narratives lost to history until recently, he introduces them as specifically American, expressing what the co-founder of the National Association of Colored Women in 1895 called the 'unnaturally suppressed inner lives which our people have been compelled to lead'.[43] It is in this sense that Sally Hemings has touched the imaginations of those writers of fiction and of screenplays who reinstate her as a peculiarly American foremother. Her position outside of public record has rendered her especially appealing to those enquiring into alienation and citizenship. Unlike Thomas Jefferson, Sally Hemings remains an obscure alien presence in American official history but she is becoming a powerful presence in fiction and film, in ways which dramatise the relationship between race and rights as an interracial drama of American nationhood.

Notes

1. Frederick Douglass, 'What to the Slave is the Fourth of July', Independence Day speech, New York, 1852, in Philip S. Fouer (ed.), *Frederick Douglass: Selections from his Writings* (New York, International Publishers, 1964), p. 52.
2. Barbara Chase-Riboud, *The President's Daughter* (New York: Ballantine Books, 1995), p. 327.
3. Thomas Jefferson in *Jefferson in Paris* (Merchant/Ivory, 1995).
4. Thomas Jefferson, Letter to Francis Grey, 4 March 1815 cited in Annette Gordon-Reed, *Thomas Jefferson and Sally Hemings: An American Controversy* (Charlottesville and London: University Press of Virginia, 1997), p. 53 and Werner Sollors, *Neither Black Nor White Yet Both: Thematic Explorations of Interracial Literature* (New York and Oxford: Oxford University Press, 1997), pp. 113–15.
5. Contradictory readings of the Jefferson–Hemings relationship persist. Some historians believe Jefferson's nephew Pater Carr to have been the father of Hemings's children; others that his brother Samuel was her lover. Virginius Dabney, a descendant of Jefferson's sister Martha Carr, published *The Jefferson Scandals: A Rebuttal* (New York: New York University Press, 1981) to refute Fawn M. Brodie's claims in *Thomas Jefferson: An Intimate History* (London: Eyre Methuen, 1974) and the debate continues.
6. Hannah Arendt, *On Revolution* (Harmondsworth: Penguin, 1979), p. 71.
7. William Wells Brown, *Clotel or The President's Daughter* (New York: Carol University Books, 1969), p. 188.
8. Ibid., p. 68.
9. Barbara Chase-Riboud, *Sally Hemings* (New York: Ballantine Books, 1994).
10. Gordon-Reed, *Thomas Jefferson,* p. 4.
11. Ralph Ellison in Ralph Ellison, William Styron, Robert Penn Warren, C. Vann Woodward, 'The Uses of History in Fiction', *The Southern Literary Journal* (1968), p. 70.
12. Barbara Chase-Riboud in Susan McHenry, '"Sally Hemings": A Key to Our National Identity', *Ms*, October 1980, p. 37.

13. Ruth Prawer Jhabvala, 'True Grit', *Guardian*, 3 June 1995, p. 37.
14. Barbara Chase-Riboud in McHenry, p. 40.
15. James Baldwin, *Notes of a Native Son* (Harmondsworth: Penguin, 1964), pp. 14, 29.
16. Colin Kidd, 'Sing Tantarara', *London Review of Books*, 30 October 1997, p. 12.
17. Wyndham Lewis, *America and Cosmic Man* (New York: Doubleday, 1949), p. 127.
18. See, for example, Lizzie Francke, *Observer*, 18 June 1995, p. 11.
19. The letter is 'To Martha Jefferson, Annapolis November 28, 1783' reproduced in Merrill D. Peterson (ed.), *The Portable Thomas Jefferson* (Harmondsworth: Penguin, 1975), pp. 366–7. It is creatively if somewhat anachronistically positioned in the film text since it preceeds Jefferson's arrival in Paris in 1784 when Martha accompanied him.
20. Nathan Huggins, *Revelations: American History, American Myths* (New York and Oxford: Oxford University Press, 1995), p. 277.
21. Myra Jehlen, *American Incarnation: The Individual, the Nation and the Continent* (Cambridge, MA and London: Harvard University Press, 1986), p. 13.
22. James Baldwin, *Notes*, p. 45. See also Sollors, *Neither Black Nor White Yet Both* for detailed readings of foundational relationships.
23. Steve Erickson, *Arc D'X* (London: Vintage, 1993), p. 282.
24. Frederick Jameson, *The Political Unconscious: Narrative as a Socially Symbolic Act* (London: Methuen, 1983), p. 9.
25. Russ Castronovo, 'Radical Configurations of History in the Era of American Slavery', *American Literature*, 65: 3 (1993), p. 523.
26. William Wells Brown, 'Narrative of the Life and Escape of William Wells Brown' in Brown, *Clotel*, pp. 17–55.
27. Judith N. Shklar, *American Citizenship: The Quest for Inclusion* (Cambridge, MA and London: Harvard University Press, 1995), p. 1.
28. Erickson, *Arc D'X*, pp. 16 and 51.

29. Ralph Ellison, *Invisible Man* (Harmondsworth: Penguin, 1965), p. 67. Harriet Beecher Stowe, *Uncle Tom's Cabin* (New York and London: Signet, 1966), p. 289.
30. Chase-Riboud, *The President's Daughter*, p. 327.
31. Chase-Riboud, *Sally Hemings*, p. 63.
32. John Quincy Adams quoted in Leonard I. Sweet, 'The Fourth of July and Black Americans in the Nineteeth Century: Northern Leadership Opinion Within the Context of the Black Experience', *Journal of Negro History*, 61: 3 (1976), pp. 256–7.
33. Sojourner Truth was in fact freed together with all other slaves in New York State exactly a year later in an unprecedented decision by the State Legislature. See, for example, Sweet, 'The Fourth of July', p. 266.
34. Chase-Riboud, *Sally Hemings*, pp. 55–60.
35. Ibid., p. 242.
36. For example, 'I Have A Dream' (1963) begins with reference to the Declaration of Independence and intones that: 'One hundred years later the Negro is still languished in the corners of American society and finds himself an exile in his own land.'
37. See Eric J. Sundquist, 'Blues for Atticus Finch: Scottsboro, *Brown* and Harper Lee' in Larry J. Griffin and Dan H. Hoyle, *The South as an American Problem* (Athens and London: University of Georgia Press, 1995), pp. 184–5.
38. Priscilla Wald, *Constituting Americans* (Durham, NC and London: Duke University Press, 1995). See especially the chapter on Frederick Douglass entitled 'Neither Citizen nor Alien' in which Wald posits an argument that differs from my own.
39. Toni Morrison, *Playing in the Dark: Whiteness and the Literary Imagination* (Cambridge, MA and London: Harvard University Press, 1992), p. 52. See also, Sharon Monteith, 'Writing for Re-Vision', *New Formations*, 20 (Summer 1993), pp. 173–80.
40. Howard McGary, 'Alienation and the African-American Experience' in John P. Pittman (ed.), *African-American Perspectives and Philosophical Traditions* (New York and London: Routledge, 1997), pp. 282–96.

41. For a development of this argument, see Hessian van Gunsteren, 'Four Conceptions of Citizenship' in Bart van Steenbergen (ed.), *The Condition of Citizenship* (London, Thousand Oaks, New Delhi: Sage, 1994), pp. 36–48.
42. Ellison, *Invisible Man*, p. 355.
43. Victoria Earle Matthews quoted by Henry Louis Gates, 'Foreword: In Her Own Write', *Six Women's Slave Narratives* (New York and Oxford: Oxford University Press, 1988), p. xv.

3

See Europe with ITC: Stock Footage and the Construction of Geographical Identity

Nick Freeman

> The past, so they say, is a foreign country
> And abroad equally.[1]

> Most of the time, geography is just an illusion, features on a map, words on a stamp. That's all it takes to give a country its real identity. After all, you're in the country that you believe yourself to be in ... countries are subjective things.[2]

It is an over-simplification to equate the 1950s with monochrome austerity and the 1960s with a new-found Technicolor luxuriance, but it is one that contains substantial elements of truth as well as enduring mythic power. Colour gave cinema an edge over the burgeoning television industry, but once the latter began to develop colour transmission the tables turned.[3] During the 1960s the television set evolved from a status symbol into a ubiquitous domestic accessory, and although colour programming was not universal in Britain until 1969 its growing visibility was demonstrated by the shift to colour of many popular series.[4] Colour seemed essential for the portrayal and marketing of 'Swinging London', a fact which television executives quickly realised. Of course, television was less quick off the mark than certain other media, notably the *Sunday Times Colour Supplement* which began publication in February 1962, but once the process was under way it was swift and irreversible.

At the same time as television became increasingly committed to colour programming, it began to broaden its geographical horizons. In the 1950s domestic television companies set most of their productions in Britain, invariably shooting in the studio as this was far cheaper than location shooting, as well as more amenable to the live performances which were often transmitted at this time. Watching the threadbare studio Sherwood of Richard Greene's *The Adventures of Robin Hood* (ATV, 1955) or the cardboard castles of Roger Moore's *Ivanhoe* (ATV, 1958) today necessitates an accommodating nostalgia, and while extremely popular, such shows quickly revealed their parochial and dated natures when seen against the slick contemporary settings of American shows of the same period, such as *Dragnet* (ITV, 1955), *I Love Lucy* (ITV, 1955), *Highway Patrol* (ITV, 1956) and *Sgt. Bilko* (BBC, 1957). Imperial Britain, whose prestige had been undermined first by the Second World War, and then by the Korean and Suez crises of the 1950s, turned back on itself, dramatising the worth of its defiantly ordinary citizens in a series of films and television shows from *The Blue Lamp* (Basil Dearden, 1949) and Ealing comedies to the documentaries of Denis Mitchell, while at the same time reaching backwards into a legendary and heroic past which valorised clear-cut moral polarities and conservative social attitudes. There were exceptions of course, notably *Interpol Calling* (ATV, 1959), but the basic point remains valid.

The appearance of Ian Fleming's James Bond marks the beginning of a shift away from these tendencies, although as many have shown, the Bond ethos is itself conservative in many respects. While the first Bond film, *Dr. No* (Terence Young), was not released until 1962, Fleming's flamboyant agent moved away from the seediness and gloom of *The Third Man* (Carol Reed, 1949) into a brightly lit world of sunshine, roulette wheels, stylish machinery and glamorous, sexually available women. Bond could not exist in a monochrome milieu, despite his first appearance having been in a television version of *Casino Royale*; neither could he be found in the grubby Viennese back streets of Graham Greene's screenplay. Bond's arenas and playgrounds were the Riviera and the Caribbean, environments which were unfamiliar to the overwhelming majority of the novels' original readership but consequently richly evocative and appealing. While Fleming was quickly countered by writers determined to maintain a deliberately down-beat and anti-heroic tradition of spy fiction, Bond's popularity could hardly fail to escape the attention of television companies.

The rise of Bond was of enormous significance for television in the 1960s. The novels' cocktail of chic brutality, sexual licence and stylish consumer totems seemed inherently cinematic, while Bond himself exemplified many mythic characteristics, locating him in an older heroic context even as he represented a fresh perspective upon it. However, just as he could not exist in black-and-white, so his particular brand of heroism required if not a global then at least an exotic theatre. In the Bond films and the television series which they inspired, British audiences came face to face with the alien worlds of Europe and beyond in a way they had rarely experienced before. In the process of this cultural re-envisioning, intriguing new light would be thrown on Britain's perception of itself and others.

The expectation of exoticism in Bond may have been increased by the significant growth of foreign holidaying from the mid-1960s. The late Victorian era had seen the rise of specific holiday companies such as Thomas Cook, which offered more affordable trips to the continent than ever before. Before the First World War, France and Italy in particular were becoming favourite destinations for middle-class travellers, a suggestion supported by the proliferation of cheap travel guides and the appearance of 'tourists' in the fiction of Henry James, E.M. Forster and others. The depression of the 1930s, the Second World War and the decade of reconstruction following it slowed the development of twentieth-century tourism beyond the social elite which had savoured it since the days of the Grand Tour, but by the mid-1960s the holiday trade was at once recovering and diversifying as never before. The growth of the affordable 'package', a trip to purpose-built resorts or a guided tour, continued throughout the decade and into the 1970s, and was also a two-way process, with European and American tourists visiting the United Kingdom in unprecedented numbers. Mel Stuart's *If It's Tuesday, This Must be Belgium* (1969) dramatised some of the wide-ranging cultural consequences of European exploration in its concern with the crazily paced coach tour. These consequences are further encompassed in both Britain's on-off affair with the Common Market (1961–75) and the 'low' comedy of *Carry On Abroad* (Gerald Thomas, 1972), the 'hippie' rejection of organised tourism, a practice which itself led to the creation of established 'trails', and the proliferation of foreign characters, invariably though by no means always attractive young women, fulfilling the roles of sexually liberated *au pairs* or students in situation comedies, most notoriously in *Mind Your Language* (LWT, 1977–79).

For television, a key side-effect of these processes was an increased audience familiarity with notions of 'abroad'. This is not to suggest that many viewers had actually travelled to Europe or beyond, as the percentage of Britons taking foreign holidays remained small, and the invaluable monitoring of HMSO's *Social Trends* series did not begin until 1970. However, awareness of what the wider world offered was far greater than in previous eras. It may be glib to claim that stereotypes founded upon ignorance were confirmed by those derived from familiarity, but it is tempting to suggest that British pre-conceptions of the foreign were constantly reinforced in characterisations such as the seedy, treacherous Arab, the lecherous though stylish Italian and the American who boasts technological superiority but lacks British (or more specifically, English) 'pluck' and cunning.

News coverage of the Second World War, together with the travel opportunities enforced by mass mobilisation had initiated this process, but it had been accelerated by the break up of the Empire and the beginnings of substantial Commonwealth immigration during the 1950s, which had also alerted the domestic market to cultural difference in many ways. Increasing British involvement in European sport, especially football, was another important element in famil-iarisation, with growing numbers of fans leaving Britain both for international matches and cup competitions. Perhaps the most significant informative influence of all though was the media. The 1960s began with the growth of the colour supplement and 'glossies', combined with governmental support for colour television in the 1962 Pilkington Report; the decade ended with the beginning of leisure television programming such as *Holiday* (BBC1, 1969). These factors combined with a variety of others, such as the increased 'glob-alisation' of school geography curricula and the diversification of internationally inspired food outlets such as Pizzaland, founded in 1969, to create a viewing public to which television had to respond, especially as it had been responsible in many respects for its creation.

The literary and cinematic popularity of Bond, combined with the steady proliferation of viewers who possessed knowledge of elements of his world, was increasingly difficult for existing programming to accommodate. An immediate consequence was a splitting of crime-based shows into domestic police dramas, such as *Dixon of Dock Green* (BBC, 1955) and *Z Cars* (BBC, 1962), which showed everyday police work with ever increasing 'realistic' elements, and interna-tionally set series, which offered the combined appeal of exciting narrative continental colour. The prototypes for the latter were the Bond industry, and the older playboy protagonist Simon Templar of Leslie Charteris's Saint novels. The Saint had first appeared in *Meet the Tiger* (1928) and had been a popular film character since the 1930s, incarnated by actors such as Lewis Hayward, George Sanders and even Vincent Price. However, when Roger Moore tired of tights and cardboard shields in 1958, Robert S. Baker, Monty Berman and Lew Grade were quick to see the potential for a Saint television series. This began on ITV in 1962, initially in black and white, but becoming colour in 1966.

Adventurers rather than detectives, Bond and Templar were not tied to one place. They could travel to seek out criminal elements, or, as in the case of *The Saint*, also exploit serendipity. This geographical flexibility allowed writers to decorate well-known plotlines with dashes of local colour, but it posed one overwhelming problem for television production, namely, the invariably prohibitive financial cost of location filming. The solutions to this problem raise a number of questions, which this chapter seeks to address.

The obvious answer to the problem of expense was to employ library footage, shot throughout the world and tradi-tionally popular in advertising and cinema. It was cheap, plentiful and allowed scene-setting with a minimum of exposition. Unfortunately, it was difficult to integrate into a dramatic context, chiefly because it could not, by definition, feature the actors appearing in the series into which it was imported. Thus it was forced to remain a background detail, and was relegated to establishing shots. Throughout the 1960s and 1970s, directors and production companies had frequent recourse to it, to the extent that certain sequences recur with remarkable regularity, notably the 'ITC owl' and 'white Jaguar' footage discussed by Geoff Tibballs in his guide to *Randall & Hopkirk Deceased*.[5] When a warehouse caught fire close to Elstree Studios, Monty Berman filmed it in the hope that it might be of use in the future – it was! These familiar snippets are obviously the result of tight production schedules and a determination to reduce costs, and as such do not represent a significant ideological statement. Location footage, however, was rather different.

Theatre has always accepted and exploited its artificiality. The most sumptuous production of *Antony and Cleopatra* cannot hope to offer more than a suggestion of Rome and Alexandria: consequently, writers, actors, directors and designers combine to offer illusions of varying sophistication and complexity. In essence, the audience is asked to accept what it knows to be untrue in order to focus interest on the piece in performance; rather than question its commitment to verisimilitude, viewers suspend their disbelief. Television has far greater resources than theatre at its disposal, not least because it can exploit the 'real' in its dramatisation of the fictional. Whether or not an audience believes Simon Templar exists outside books and films is secondary, since his avatar can be seen outside the Houses of Parliament or standing in Piccadilly Circus. Stock footage problematises this process because it allows an interjection of objective or apparently 'neutral' library film – the Eiffel Tower, a Jamaican beach – into the determinedly 'unreal' dramatic events for which it provides a backdrop. 'Real life', in other words, is co-opted by the televisual and recontextualised in terms of the fictive. The effect is all the more odd by often being signalled either by a Hitchcockian contempt for realism or sheer incompetence – *Department S* (ATV/ITC, 1968) regularly cuts from footage which seems to have been shot on differing film stock from that of the parent programme to creakingly obvious sets, notably the square of beach which symbolises and serves as the Riviera. The action is positioned in what amounts almost to a Foucauldian *espace autre*, an often bewildering liminal zone which is at once 'set', 'setting' and the 'real' place invoked in the interests of narratorial accuracy.

Stock footage represented a deliberate attempt to shape the viewer's response to international locations. While some of these are a legacy of the imperialistic shorthand of schoolboy fiction, perceptively noted by George Orwell in 'Boys' Weeklies' (1939), others reveal much about more recent British attitudes to Europe and the wider world.[6] As noted above, British writers before the First World War had relished the narrative opportunities generated by tourism. The tourist is, by definition, never in one place long enough to thoroughly assimilate its modes of behaviour, and the consequence is a series of failures to adapt to alien mores which may be comic or more tragic depending upon the needs or conventions of the novel. Tourists themselves are largely absent from the adventure series of the 1960s and 1970s, essentially because everyday people do not belong in their mythic universe. Nonetheless, the paraphernalia of tourism loomed large, with airports acting as initiatory gateways for plots (mistaken identity is a favourite) and with frequent footage of jet airliners, one of the major technological marvels of the period.

It was through the use of the jet airliner that the escapist strategy and rationale of the holiday met that of the adventure series. The jet opened up Europe to British travellers and businessmen as never before, with Paris, Rome and Geneva, three favourite settings for adventures, within easy reach. Television presented European capitals through the techniques of the holiday brochure, establishing a series of shorthand references to place which could then be abandoned once the narrative got properly underway. An episode of *The Saint* for example might symbolise Paris through the use of stock footage of the Eiffel Tower and a hint of accordion on the soundtrack, before showing Simon Templar facing the intrigues viewers expected in one of his adventures. Rome was traditionally evoked with a shot of a traffic jam and the Coliseum, Geneva with either a pan across the lake or the sight of clean, modern office buildings; the credits for *The Champions* (ITC, 1967) use both.

The ITC adventure series of the 1960s and 1970s, from *Danger Man* (1960) to *Jason King* (1972), made location footage an essential part of many of their narratives. Of 118 episodes of *The Saint*, less than half were set in Britain. Templar frequently surfaced in Paris, Rome or on the Riviera, as well as in more far flung (and admittedly unlikely) environments such as Peru and Australia. In the case of distant surroundings, the production team opted for impressionist renderings of locale, with cicada drenched soundtracks signifying the hot tropical nights, and Roger Moore's wardrobe appropriately tailored to climatic extremes. With few of the UK audience in a position to contradict what they saw, and with foreign sales to such countries less important than the core markets of Britain, Europe and America, ITC did not feel constrained by the obligations of verisimilitude.[7]

The treatment of European cities was very different. Here ITC faced a much higher level of audience knowledge, an increasing body of which was drawn from personal acquaintance with Paris, Rome, Geneva and Amsterdam. The generic conventions of the series may have combined the thriller with fantasy elements, but that did not mean that the producers could afford to patronise the public by offering an Elstree lot disguised as the Champs Elysées. It was in such cases that the use of location footage became a political device as well as an economy measure.

Watching any ITC series of this period, one quickly becomes aware of the complex tensions between audience expectations, narrative, setting and directorial ingenuity. Directors find themselves having to suggest place with a minimum of resources and air-time. Episodes of *The Saint* took between ten and fourteen days to produce, so there was never time for much trickery or post-production smoothing of rough edges. In this environment, directors had to convince an audience that the Saint was in Paris, often without being able to show him being there. One solution was to begin an episode with a bold establishing shot, almost akin to a theatrical backdrop, a technique long familiar in cinema. In such cases, London (or even England) would be symbolised by Parliament and the

Thames, almost as if there was an internationally agreed set of representational gestures which employed conservative picture-postcard imagery to evoke the essence of the country portrayed. The point was drummed home either by on-screen captions, or by Roger Moore's opening address to camera. *Department S* used its pre-*The X Files* (Fox, 1993) pseudo-scientific exactitude to give precise details of setting and date, while the later spin-off *Jason King* was set in the French capital, where King (Peter Wyngarde) lived the flamboyant life of a tax exile. Episodes invariably began with a shot of the Arc de Triomphe.

Having established the location, the next step was to embark on a process of what might be termed reinforcement through narrative detail. The script would make strenuous attempts to mention the setting at regular intervals. The *Department S* episode 'The Mysterious Man in the Flying Machine' (1969) opens with a caption, 'Paris, March 8th', and its opening dialogue is a gendarme intoning 'il est morte' over a corpse – however, nobody else bothers to speak in French except when King orders another drink in a bar with a swift 'Encore!' In 'A Thin Band of Air' (1972), Jason King wishes his cleaning lady 'Bonjour Mademoiselle' but speaks only a few lines of French to his visitors even though the story is set in Paris. The full panoply of accents is employed by the supporting cast, who are often augmented by 'genuine' Europeans in minor roles. Characters remain closeted in bars, cafes, restaurants and houses where the illusion of 'abroad' can be maintained relatively easily. If they have to venture outside, they are either never seen in traffic or moving through recognisable environments – *Department S* and *Jason King* regularly use a particular stretch of deserted road to represent everything from Umbrian countryside to the A4 – or else travel is suggested by means of further stock footage, typically night shots of Montmartre or Leicester Square, or an airliner (usually the same Pan-Am Boeing 747) taking off from a sun-drenched but anonymous airport.

These tactics allowed the creation of locations which were at once topographically recognisable and fantastically alien. Paris, in these episodes, is simultaneously present, through the constant parade of references to it, the glimpses of identifiable landmarks and details, and absent, since it exists not as a physical environment but a form of implication, a dramatic shorthand through which it is suggested everywhere but never inhabited. In his fascinating analysis of *Danger Man*, David Buxton connects 'the positioning shots of London and other capitals like Cairo, Rome, or Singapore which begin most episodes, perhaps intended to reinforce the difference between dangerous foreign cities and London, where diverse world wrongs could begin to be put right' with what he terms 'a nod to pop's cosmopolitanism in which the foreign is a condition of excitement'.[8] Without disagreeing entirely with this observation, in wider terms London itself is frequently rendered in the same terms as Paris or other foreign cities. Its visual and imaginative instability, occasionally shored up by rhubarbing Cockney extras and gratuitous shots of tourist attractions, designed to attract domestic as well as foreign attention, make it far from the stable reference point Buxton posits, or that the narratives themselves seem to require. This effect is even more noticeable in colour series, often because of the disjointed nature of stock inserts, their anachronistic fashions, and so on.

The great cities of Europe metamorphose through such treatment into treacherous images of themselves. If, for the nineteenth-century Austrian minister Metternich, Italy was 'a mere geographical expression', in these series it becomes no more than a set of imaginative associations endlessly alluding to another country altogether. The 'Italy' imagined by British script-writers and directors is a transferable set of signs carrying with it preconceived associations which are exploited in the interests of narrative, rather than that inhabited by millions of Italians or delineated in atlases and gazetteers. However, it could be argued that in choosing to portray Europe and Britain, specifically London, in these ways, the series was echoing, consciously or not, the very images of these places that were appearing in holiday advertisements, magazine features and other television shows which may have used similar footage in the first place. As a consequence of such strategies, places are evoked in terms of a media-impelled circularity which becomes increasingly removed from notions of 'authenticity'. This does, however, allow the media's consumers to forge an identification between themselves and the glamorous, jet-setting protagonists of the series. Both can, in essence, 'see' the same 'Paris', that is, experience it through a series of stylised facsimiles. The reproduction of national symbols to encourage inference of the whole had always been a popular technique of travel writers, but it could be put to more radical uses. In *A Rebours* (1884) J.K. Huysmans creates a virtual London for Des Esseintes in a French Channel coast pub crammed with English trippers, while Len Deighton's *The Ipcress File* (1962) employs all the paraphernalia of a labour camp in an effort to convince Harry Palmer that he is in Eastern Europe while he is actually in central London. The fake England of *Danger Man*'s 'Colony Three' and the stylised Village of *The Prisoner* (ITV, 1967–8) are further variations on this theme and, like Deighton's, are imbued with the oppressive suspicions of the Cold War. In these instances setting reinforces the daring of the McGoohan characters, who are quite often alone in disorienting or hostile environments. *The Saint, Department S, The Champions* and *Jason King* are less sinister and thought provoking than the McGoohan series, less likely to employ the *leitmotivs* of paranoia and alienation, but they draw upon similar techniques in constructing their versions of 'France' or 'The Caribbean'.

This embracing of artificiality by the shows' writers makes the situation yet more complex. Already subject to budgetary considerations which rendered time 'on location' minimal, *Department S* excelled in presenting fakes, facsimiles and deceptive parallels. 'The Mysterious Man in the Flying Machine' begins with a shooting in an airliner, after which the assassin jumps from the 'plane', revealed to be a mocked-up fuselage in a warehouse.[9] In such circumstances the programme's anti-realistic elements became a defiant celebration of the possibilities of writerly ingenuity, rather than the generic obligations of a simple 'mystery' series. If the puzzles presented are, initially at least, unfathomable, it is no surprise and very possibly to their advantage that their setting is concomitantly disorienting.

Without detailed accounts of the audiences for such shows, it is difficult to discuss how they were perceived when originally transmitted, and the waters have been further muddied by their regular revival as kitsch curios on Saturday afternoon or cable television. Nonetheless, it seems likely that *The Saint*, *Department S* and *Jason King* appealed to several types of viewer: excitable small children, leering dads drawn to cars and 'disposable darling' supporting players, and the female viewers who threatened to submerge Joel Fabiani, Peter Wyngarde and Roger Moore beneath tides of fan mail. As entertainment, shown during prime time on independent television, the shows made few bids for an up-market sophisticated audience, although that in no way implies that their aficionados lacked discernment.

Discussing his ITC work in a 1995 documentary, Peter Wyngarde claimed to be aware of the problems of cost-cutting, apparently telling the producers: 'we've got to go on more locations, we must stop using this terrible back thing [back-projection] with me in the car. The audience are not fooled. You can't fool the audience.'[10] Admittedly, no audience likes to be patronised, or offered the obviously shoddy, but Wyngarde's comments underestimate the critical sensibilities of viewers capable of switching from guffawing disbelief to nonetheless wholehearted enjoyment of the programme. ITC series employed startlingly unconvincing day-for-night shots, as well as the full range of studio trickery, from wobbly back-projection and obvious models to polystyrene snow. Although even the Bond films were not immune from these effects in their early days – witness the creaky back-projection of Venice at the end of *From Russia With Love* (Terence Young, 1963) – television embraced them with reckless enthusiasm. The programmes satisfied a desire for fantasy and escapism which was intensified rather than compromised by inadequate mimetics. Stock footage was accepted by viewers as a narrative convention equivalent to the traditional use of metonymic theatrical staging, but had at the same time ideological overtones which reached beyond the pleasure of spotting continuity errors or deriding haphazard matte work. It should also be noted that even when *Jason King* used genuine location footage, it frequently looked no more convincing than the obviously bogus material, and further distinctions have to be made between location filming of actual locations, and that which used the Surrey or Berkshire countryside as Switzerland or Greece.

Stock footage established a disconcerting, destabilised context for credulity-straining adventure. It created a virtual Europe of bars, beaches, famous monuments, hotels, airports and grand mansions, one which was traversed in style in King's Bentley or the elegant Volvo P1800 driven by the Saint, but one which also kept the playboy protagonist at one remove from the ordinary. The narratives' seamless transitions from airport to hotel to beach mirrored the organisational shape of the package holiday, as did many of the destinations featured in the programmes of the mid-1960s onwards. There was also little sense of continuity between adventures, with Simon Templar in particular visiting one destination after another with little sense of cumulative experience. Stock footage reinforced these suggestions of vacation and unreality, and it is tempting to suggest that just as package holidays could never hope to reveal the 'authentic' qualities of their destinations, offering instead a consumable encounter with elements of England transferred to a meteorologically advantageous locale (hence the profusion of 'English pubs' on the Costa Brava), so these series are televisual analogues to the holiday brochure: a collection of misleading, artificial visions designed to entice briefly and then, once invested in, be forgotten despite their incidental pleasures. It is perhaps telling that *The Persuaders!* (ITC, 1971) could not employ stock footage, as its playboy heroes were on permanent Mediterranean holiday. As rich, independent men-of-the-world they could be witnessed sunning themselves in the casino culture of Monte Carlo rather than having that world evoked through televisual sleight-of-hand. *The Persuaders!'* financial backing meant that it did not need to resort to stock shots, but more importantly, it could not afford to, so important was the setting to its *mise en scène*. Danny Wilde and Lord Brett Sinclair were tax exiles, revelling in conspicuous consumption. To cut corners in production would have cheapened the entire ethos of the show, one reason why it was the most expensive British television series of its period.[11]

Jean Baudrillard has written at length on the age of the simulacrum, in which codes have superseded signs and in which the difference between the real and the reproduction is erased. Without wishing to claim that the television series discussed here were harbingers of this postmodernity, to analyse them now is to become aware of how in manipulating the set of associations bracketed together as Paris or Rome, they assembled symbolic locations which achieved a remarkable internal consistency through the reiteration of stock shots and other presentational techniques. Jason King, Simon Templar, the Champions, all inhabit the same Paris even though that city is not the 'real' French capital. Hyperreality has intervened, transforming the landscapes of the series into imaginative cues, gestures towards alterity and the recognisable vistas of the brochure or Sunday supplement article. Nowhere is this better illustrated than in a late episode of *Jason King*, 'Uneasy Lies the Head' (1972), written by Donald James and directed by Cyril Frankel.

The episode's plot concerns an attempt by various international intelligence agencies to counteract a Turkish drug cartel. Its semi-surreal plot details, which involve Lance Percival's British agent impersonating King in order to instil a sense of socio-political responsibility in the dilettante novelist, are less important than its treatment of setting. The pre-credit sequence features a shot of minarets and the Bosphorus by night, accompanied by the calling of a muezzin. This cuts to a warehouse, which looks disconcertingly similar to the one used in previous episodes set in Paris and Berlin. After some violent activity, the scene changes to London, introduced by overhead stock images of Parliament and the River Thames. This is followed by a close-up of a street sign reading Whitehall, and a shot of the Cenotaph, before cutting to a meeting in a Whitehall office. The next setting is a beauty salon, supposedly in France, but clearly recognisable as the 'Italian' chateau from 'The Company I Keep' (1971), another episode in the series. There is the obligatory use of the Pan-Am 747, before further establishing shots of Paris, evoked through a cross-city view of the Eiffel Tower. There is also a sequence purporting to involve the road to Fontainebleau, although this again looks very like the road to the chateau in 'The Company I Keep', not to mention a Spanish track from a *Department S* episode. While this assemblage succeeds in giving the narrative an international dialogue between Turkey, England and France, it also serves to confuse the boundaries between the three countries. The episode serves up hoary national stereotypes while at the same time suggesting the new era of European co-operation. Typically, it is the Turks who are treacherous, and British ingenuity and courage win out.

'Uneasy Lies the Head' transforms Turkey into an exotic, performative construction in which Western distrust of Orientalism is combined with spatial mutability. Watched passively, using the establishing shots as taken-as-read theatrical devices, the show is an intermittently amusing adventure. However, examined in terms of its use of destabilised national parameters, it becomes altogether more complex, giving an intriguing slant to Britain's view of Europe in the early 1970s through its dramatic form and technical content as much as through the attitudes of its screenplay. What might have become a bold televisual exploration of an unfamiliar country instead becomes a xenophobic invocation of national stereotypes, which bear as much resemblance to the actual Turkey as the Old Kent Road does to Monte Carlo.

In showing these series, contemporary television tends to relish an ironised distance between past and present. BBC2's 'A Day in the Sixties', transmitted in August 1993, selected *Department S* for affectionate ridicule, noting that episodes began in Paris or Jamaica but returned to the Home Counties when the stock footage ran out. While it is possible to restrict one's engagement with the shows to this level of flip cynicism, they reveal much about British television's attitudes towards itself and the wider world. As the British involvement in European economic and cultural affairs increased, so Europeans began to be portrayed more positively. Nonetheless, the vision of Europe encapsulated in the ITC series of the late 1960s is one which rarely strays from the beaten track. In terms of the wider world, imperial habits die harder, with blacked-up African despots and dictators of banana republics being both corrupt and stupid. The relationship with America is the most problematic of all – one reason why these series frequently import and uneasily assimilate Americans into European or domestic adventures, rather than seeing British characters overwhelmed by the United States in a disquieting echo of post-war realities. By using stock footage to maintain fixed images of places and people, ITC was able to establish some sort of stasis in a world of rapid change, and keep the uncomfortably 'other' in its place. Fundamentally conservative, they replayed older stereotypes for the age of the package tour before deciding that Paris or Rome might be lovely places for holidays, but there was no place like home.

Notes

All dates for programmes refer to the commencing of original transmissions and the channel on which the series was first shown.

1. Nicholas Currie, 'The Rape of Lucrece', *Lusts for a Moron: The Complete Poems of Manns* (London: Black Spring Press, 1992), p. 44.
2. 'Colony Three', *Danger Man* (ITV, 1965), quoted in David Buxton, *From The Avengers to Miami Vice: Form and Ideology in Television Series* (Manchester: Manchester University Press, 1990), p. 89.
3. For a detailed account of the movement from monochrome to colour, and the threat to the film industry from television, see Robert Murphy, *Sixties British Cinema* (London: British Film Institute, 1992).
4. The BBC began experimental colour transmissions (chiefly still images, demonstration films and some basic studio shots) in October 1955. By December 1959, licences had been issued for 10 million combined television and sound receiving sets. This number has increased steadily since that date. See Tise Vahimagi, *British Television: An Illustrated Guide* (Oxford: Oxford University Press, 1994).
5. Geoff Tibballs, *Randall & Hopkirk Deceased* (London: Boxtree, 1994), pp. 29–30.
6. George Orwell, 'Boys' Weeklies', *Critical Essays* (London: Secker and Warburg, 1946).
7. Only one episode of *The Saint*, 'The Loving Brothers' (b/w, 1964) had an Australian setting. Its depictions of Australians are stereotypical and few efforts are made to give the setting anything beyond a superficial coating of antipodean mannerism. The show may have been a

success in Australia precisely because it tended to avoid Australian settings. ITC was always willing to sell its shows to English-speaking countries, and *Department S* enjoyed phenomenal popularity 'down under'. Sales to South America mattered less – perhaps one reason for the often hideously xenophobic story lines, or, as with Africa, references to non-existent countries. See Tony Mechele and Dick Fiddy, *The Saint* (London: Boxtree, 1989).

8. Buxton, *From The Avengers to Miami Vice*, p. 92. For detailed critical comment see Toby Miller, *The Avengers* (London: British Film Institute, 1997).

9. *The Avengers* took this inventiveness to astonishing extremes, but its largely English settings and relish of unlikely interiors place it beyond the scope of this chapter.

10. Wyngarde made his remarks in an interview during *The Cult Corporation* (Bravo, 1995).

11. For an interesting reading of this series and *Jason King* in terms of the economic changes of the period, see Leon Hunt, *British Low Culture: From Safari Suits to Sexploitation* (London: Routledge, 1998), pp. 65–73. Lew Grade was so determined to make *The Persuaders!* that he managed to get Tony Curtis to renounce his vow not to do television work, as well as succeeding in postponing Moore's transition to full-time film acting.

4

'Leaving the West and Entering the East': Refiguring the Alien from Stoker to Coppola

Paul O'Flinn

Dracula, along with *Frankenstein* and *The Strange Case of Dr Jekyll and Mr Hyde*, is one of a curious group of nineteenth-century texts that live in powerful if weirdly mutated forms in twentieth-century culture. Even though the novel has never been out of print since its publication in 1897, most people have not read it. Indeed, many would be pressed to remember the name of its author Bram Stoker who appears as little more than an extended footnote in traditional academic histories of fiction. And yet Dracula still drifts across our fantasies and nightmares, his face snarls from adverts and breakfast cereal packets, his cape flaps across television screens and sweet wrappers.

Why has this figure avoided the rapid death that awaits the cardboard bogeymen of the dozens of cheap horror novels that are published every year? Why has he persisted as the undead, transformed into a modern myth, a small but significant element in the shaping and the socialisation of the desires and terrors of people living a century after Stoker wrote the book? The answer to these questions is in cultural terms enormously important. Importance lies partly in the centrality of the horror genre in the cultural life of young people: a survey by the booksellers Waterstones found that 70 per cent of teenage girls and 65 per cent of boys read horror novels.[1] Estimates of the number of films made worldwide in the past seventy years based on *Dracula* go as high as 400.[2] What are the reasons for this massive phenomenon, what are the economic forces that shape it, the ideologies that guide it and the truths about our society that such proliferation suggests?

People live through the stories that constitute a culture. The songs we listen to and sing, the tales we hear and tell help to make a consoling sense of the jumble of stimuli and demands that press daily on our lives. Together we create an ambience that expresses and develops but also limits and determines our imaginations and aspirations. The point of balance between these twin roles of culture – as free expression of a people on the one hand and as a process by which we are ruled and repressed on the other – is extremely difficult to determine and not made easier by the fact that that point is never still and moves even as we try to locate it.

When trying to think clearly about this problem, we need of course to start with Marx. (The fact that everyone is doing that in the late 1990s means that one risks being accused of mere intellectual trendiness, but the results usually make the charge bearable.) People, Marx argues,

> make their own history, but they do not make it just as they please; they do not make it under circumstances chosen by themselves, but under circumstances directly encountered, given and transmitted from the past. The tradition of all the dead generations weighs like a nightmare on the brain of the living.[3]

Marx's sense of priorities – first the making, but making always in a shaping context – and their dialectical interaction helps avoid two pitfalls that scar much of the discussion of the role of culture in the socialisation of individuals. On the one hand, it guards us against the repressive hysteria that frequently characterises discussion of such things as video nasties. Such discussion implies that people are one-dimensional, passively determined by the cultural products they consume, products which therefore need to be closely monitored and censored. But on the other hand Marx also helps to escape an uneasy liberal opposition to that censorship which would seek to minimise the impact of this material to such an extent that, were it the case, the investment in its production and distribution would become pointless and indeed inexplicable. In thinking therefore about Dracula and his place in our culture we need to begin with that sense of people constantly remaking the meanings by which they live, taking hold of the stories they inherit and boldly hacking them into new shapes to articulate new realities. And yet that remaking is always more or less constrained by the circumstances in which it occurs, the openings and the barriers of the contexts in which it happens. In this chapter I shall examine those processes at work inside the history of just one of the stories in our culture.

To do that in the space of a short chapter means being highly selective. I shall begin by saying a few things about the text itself, because its curious form seems to me highly ideologically significant. Then I will focus on just one of the many film versions, namely, *Bram Stoker's Dracula*, released in 1992 by Columbia and directed by Francis Ford Coppola. I have chosen it because, as I will try to show, it occurs at a particular historical conjuncture with which it is tellingly intertwined.

What I hope to arrive at through an examination of these cultural practices from an essentially Marxist perspective is an understanding that is more profound and politically sharper than the thin or question-begging accounts currently on offer. Christopher Frayling, for example, suggests that the persistence of the story is based on 'nostalgia for the trimmings ... laced with magic ritual' while David Punter gestures towards 'some inner social and cultural dynamic which makes it necessary for these images to be kept alive'. Most explanations echo Phyllis Roth's insistence on 'the fact of the novel's sounding a near universal chord of fantasy and anxiety'.[4] What all of these accounts miss is the fact that these images and the story that contains them do not persist in an archetypal, unchanging way. Every telling is a remaking, as the old terms are smashed up and reassembled to enable them to address new fears and new desires. (Incidentally, this is one of the reasons why most old horror films which had people hiding under their seats in their day strike the average viewer as camp, comic or crap when they turn up on television forty years later.)

The other danger that flows from an insistence on the universality of the original text is that it then becomes a sacred icon, to be faithfully preserved and reproduced only with gentle reverence. Hence Clive Leatherdale's lament at the way that *Dracula* is 'habitually trivialised by the creation of the cinema' and at 'the cinema's prurient debasement of Stoker's novel', or Daniel Farson's grumble that modern versions aren't 'faithful to Stoker's original'.[5] What I hope to arrive at instead is neither on the one hand a groan of despair at the failure of the twentieth century to get Stoker's story right nor on the other a depoliticised deconstructionist delight at the way the tale can be made to mean anything and everything and nothing. Rather, the truth is that Stoker used a mass of material he inherited and discovered to make a certain kind of statement in 1897, which statement was then broken down and reassembled to speak to the different realities of 1992.

Bram Stoker's *Dracula* was published in 1897 by Archibald Constable of London, priced six shillings. Even though the collapse of the expensive three-decker novel format in the early 1890s paved the way for this relatively cheap single-volume first edition, it is still true to say that in terms both of medium and of genre the early readers would have been drawn predominantly from the British middle classes and it was middle-class British journals that first reviewed it.[6] What strikes a reader now is the silence of those first reviews on the subject of the disturbing, highly erotic sexual messages that the text sends out. That silence has in the last few years been broken by a roar of academic voices; there is no need to add to that roar because it does more than justice to a subject which for the moment seems to me limp with exhaustion.[7] Instead, I shall focus on the specific narrative structuring of *Dracula*, an area of the text that has been relatively neglected and yet which is in the end as ideologically important as the text's overt messages about sexuality.

The examination of that structuring makes sense if we start where every reader starts, namely, the beginning: the list of contents, the dedication, the author's brief introductory note, the first page. An immense amount happens in those opening moments when the text first hails its readers and positions them as subjects. The list of contents, for example, doesn't suggest a novel at all. The chapter titles promise extracts from the journals, letters and diaries of four men and women as well as a precisely dated newspaper cutting. What we are apparently offered is a variety of non-fictional forms from a variety of subject positions. This sense of an attempt to arrive at objective, historical truth by means of a carefully assembled catalogue of authentic contemporary documents is reinforced by a brief opening note. It is unattributed and therefore presumably the work of the author who scrupulously absents himself from the rest of the texts that he hands over to a series of witnesses. The note reads in full:

> How these papers have been placed in sequence will be made manifest in the reading of them. All needless matters have been eliminated, so that a history almost at variance with the possibilities of later-day [*sic*] belief may stand forth as simple fact. There is throughout no statement of past things wherein memory may err, for all the records chosen are exactly contemporary, given from the standpoints and within the range of knowledge of those who made them.[8]

At one level these are simply the conventional feints of realist fiction, a device that acts out an opening pretence of historical truth both to lend authenticity to the narrative and also to ease any feelings of bourgeois guilt that might be associated with time spent reading mere stories.

However, it is not enough simply to register a convention. The real question is why, at this relatively advanced stage of the novel's development, Stoker chose this particular convention from the many available to set his fiction moving. We can begin to see a possible answer in the opening paragraph of the story:

> Jonathan Harker's Journal
> (*Kept in shorthand*)
> *3 May. Bistritz.* – Left Munich at 8.35 p.m. on 1st May, arriving at Vienna early next morning; should have arrived at 6.46, but train was an hour late. Buda-Pesth seems a wonderful place, from the glimpse which I got of it from the train and the little I could walk through the streets. I feared to go very far from the station, as we had arrived late and would start as near the correct time as possible. The impression I had was that we were leaving the West and entering the East; the most Western of splendid bridges over the Danube, which is here of noble width and depth, took us among the traditions of Turkish rule.[9]

Again we note the typical moves of realist fiction, that exact precision about date, time and place which had been part of every novelist's equipment since the early eighteenth century. The core around which this attempt at verisimilitude circles, the notion that it seeks to establish, seems to me to be the claim that 'we were leaving the West and entering the East'.

This move from West to East, from civilisation to its alien other, from the known and the controllable to the foreign and the recalcitrant, is the characteristic strategy that initiates Stoker's fictions again and again. *The Lady of the Shroud* (1909) drops its Anglo-Irish hero Rupert Sent Leger into the nightmare of Balkan politics. There are many similar examples in *Dracula's Guest* (1914), his posthumous volume of short stories. In the first sentence of the title piece, the English narrator leaves 'the sun ... shining brightly on Munich'[10] to meet the terrors of a deserted village on Walpurgis Nacht. The first sentence of 'The Judge's House' tells us that 'Malcolm Malcolmson made up his mind to go somewhere to read by himself'[11] which decision takes him to his death in a remote haunted house. In 'The Gipsy Prophecy' the chilling prophecy works itself out when the protagonists leave the comfort of a bourgeois dining room on the opening page and visit a gipsy camp. 'Leaving Paris by the Orleans road'[12] is how 'The Burial of the Rats' begins, and it is a journey that takes another English narrator from the sophistication of Paris into a paranoid fight to survive among the shanty dwellers and dustheaps of Montrouge. 'Crooken Sands' is about a London merchant who encounters 'mystery and horror'[13] when he takes his family for a holiday in the north of Scotland. Lastly, 'The Squaw' describes another middle-class English couple who, on their European honeymoon, witness a macabre killing in Nurnberg.

What is going on here, beyond the obvious suggestion that next year, my dear, we should perhaps stick to Torquay? The frequency with which Stoker makes this opening move into the alien and terrifying takes us far beyond mere coincidence and into indicative obsession. To understand that obsession we need to think about the main facts of Stoker's life.

It is on one level a typical story of nineteenth-century Irish Protestant ascendancy. He was born in 1847 at the height of the famine in relatively comfortable Clontarf and spent nearly half of his life in Ireland, not settling in England until he was thirty-one. Although a great-uncle on his mother's side, George Blake, had been hanged for his part in the rising of 1798, the family that Bram was born into were committed Unionists and his father worked as a clerk in the Secretary's office in Dublin Castle, the centre of British rule. Bram moved through Trinity College, Dublin (at that time open only to Protestants) and then followed his father into Dublin Castle to work in the Petty Sessions office. He seemed destined for a minor role oiling the wheels of the imperial machine's bureaucracy with his first book, *The Duties of Clerks of Petty Sessions in Ireland* (1879). But then he shifted into oiling the wheels of its culture with a career in London as manager of Henry Irving's Lyceum Theatre that lasted from 1878 till Irving's death in 1905. (During the twenty-seven years he worked for Irving, Stoker estimated that he wrote half a million letters on his master's behalf. Either Stoker exaggerates or he wrote an average of fifty letters a day. The imperial machine clearly needed a fierce amount of oil.) Soon after Irving's death, a stroke broke his own health and he died in 1912.[14]

It is the archetypal biography of untold numbers of Irish people and a route followed, as Glover notes, by three of Stoker's four brothers: emigration followed by decades of labour maintaining the structures of the British state, an ascendancy version of the life history of masses of his fellow Irish who in the same century helped build and service the canals, the railways, the roads and the houses of someone else's heritage. I shall argue that powerful clusters of stormily contradictory feelings emerge from this typical experience to account for the peculiar formation of Stoker's narrative. My claim in brief is that in *Dracula* Stoker offers an apparently realistic, dialogic, polyphonic text whose overt purpose is to vindicate the dominant value system of the British ruling classes, but such purpose is subverted by an alien perspective, a potent if deeply subconscious hostility to that system and its representatives.

The *Athenaeum* review of *Dracula* on 26 June 1897 was the first to find the narrative formation unsettling and concluded by condemning the book as 'wanting in the constructive art'. Many commentators since have echoed this rejection.[15] These verdicts are surprising because at first glance *Dracula* looks like a complex and highly sophisticated exercise in late Victorian narrative art. Stoker, as we have already seen, stands aside and weaves his story out of the journals, letters and diaries of four men and women. Inserted within these interlaced accounts are a wide variety of other documents such as telegrams, a ship's log, and transcriptions from shorthand notes and phonographic records. These different sources present the reader with a text that, as well as standard English, shifts between the Yorkshire, Scottish, American and working-class accents and dialects of various characters, not to mention the bizarrely fractured ideolect of the Dutch Van Helsing.

What we appear to have in *Dracula* is the kind of polyphonic text that Mikhail Bakhtin in the twentieth century has identified as one of the supreme achievements of the earlier bourgeois novel. Bakhtin celebrates such texts which reject a single authoritarian/authorial voice and instead present us with heteroglossia, a system of languages in open dialogue. Such novels are 'the expression of a Galilean perception of language, one that denies the absolutism of a single and unitary language'; they represent 'a decentralizing of the verbal-ideological world' and offer a presumption of 'fundamentally different social groups, which exist in an intense and vital interaction with other social groups'.[16] In *Dracula* what we are offered is not a single text narrated by a controlling author but rather a series of different, competing texts that leave readers to make their own meanings out of these juxtapositions.[17]

But only a slightly closer examination of the text reveals at once that in fact Stoker merely mimes what Bakhtin was later to identify as one of the progressive modes of liberal fiction, and smuggled in behind the pluralist facade of *Dracula* is a package of single-minded values. Franco Moretti has noted that all the narrative senders are British. Differences between them are differences of detail, not of substance. The result is that, as Chris Baldick has pointed out, their narratives tend to confirm rather than challenge one another. There is none of the disturbing disjunction of values that we find, for example, between Walton, Frankenstein and the monster whose three contrasting stories make up Mary Shelley's novel.[18]

Stoker's representational control, in short, is not invested in those areas of the text inhabited by the Dutch Van Helsing, the Transylvanian Dracula or the American Quincey Morris but is placed instead in its English centre where Jonathan Harker, Mina Murray, Lucy Westenra and Dr John Seward pour out their mutually reinforcing stories, their monologue that tries to pass itself off as dialogue. By the final page that monologue is undisturbed, as Morris and Dracula are both dead and the young son of Jonathan and Mina looks forward to an untroubled inheritance.

That may be where the novel ends but there is a long journey before we reach that moment. What occupies the novelist, what fills his text before that closure is reached, is the story of how Jonathan is first imprisoned and then sexually assaulted; of how Lucy is seduced by Dracula and then staked and decapitated by her husband; and of how Mina is hunted down by Dracula and made to drink his blood in a scene that powerfully suggests enforced fellatio while her unconscious husband lies impotently at her side. The text may ultimately be about the victory of the dominant values of the imperialist upper classes, but they are made to pay dearly for their triumph as the text pushes them through a series of rapes, humiliations and dismemberments on the way. The Union Jack flutters supreme on the last page but it is a flag maliciously shot to bits on the way to its final erection. If this is a dialogic text in Bakhtin's sense then its polyphony lies not at the level of its mutually supportive narrators but rather its self-contradicting author.[19]

We can go back to the series of persecutions and disasters that befall the English characters when they move away from the safety of their homes, which I noted in the *Dracula's Guest* volume. Or we can go forward to Stoker's last novel, *The Lair of the White Worm*, where a concluding flash of lightning obliterates both the major English landowner, Edgar Caswell, and his castle and also the home of Lady Arabella March. She is reduced to 'fragments ... covered with insects, worms and vermin of all kinds ... the awful smell ... was simply unbearable'.[20] Stoker fills his pages with more brutal fantasies of the devastation of the British ruling classes than were dreamt of by the wildest Fenian bomber who ever stalked across a Victorian *Punch* cartoon.

Stoker was no Fenian bomber, for all his claim in *Personal Reminiscences of Henry Irving* to have been a 'philosophical Home Ruler'[21], a position that generated considerable teasing from Sir Henry (as he became in 1895). It was a position that must have sat awkwardly with his service to the dominant culture of London for nearly three decades. It must have sat awkwardly too with the writing of imperialist fantasies such as *The Lady of the Shroud* or his short story 'The Red Stockade', which describes with bloody relish the massacre of pirates in the Straits of Malacca before the Union Jack is run up in the pirate stockade. The fact that there was in Ireland an honourable minority tradition of Protestant support for Home Rule that stretched from Wolfe Tone, leader of the rising in 1798, through to Stoker's contemporaries such as Wilde, Shaw and Yeats, made the contradictions inherent in such a position no less sharp or easy to live with.

Dracula was published in June 1897, the same month in which Stoker in his managerial role at the Lyceum presented a special matinee performance of Conan Doyle's *Waterloo* for 'representatives of Indian and colonial troops ... gathered in London for the Diamond Jubilee of Queen Victoria'.[22] That coincidence of the novel's publication and the celebration of the apogee of Empire ought to remind us of the extent to which, at one level, *Dracula* itself reruns the stalest imperial myths, in particular the notion that Dracula, like all cultivated aliens, is grateful in ways that sadly he never articulates for his own salutary destruction at the hands of morally superior British invaders. *Personal Reminiscences of Henry Irving* is a revealingly worshipful and unreflective account of the years in which, as manager of the Lyceum, Stoker participated in the rituals of the British establishment, from unctuous records of special performances for Queen Victoria at Sandringham to a dozen double-columned pages proudly listing just some of the hundreds of upper-class drones who were entertained in Irving's private dining room at the Lyceum.[23]

But yet, as I have tried to argue, dark fantasies of the humiliation of these drones can never be fully repressed, not unlike Stoker's Dublin accent which, one observer noted, tended to erupt through his English vowels when he was angry. The contradiction in Stoker's politics – part Irish nationalist, part British imperialist – is inscribed in the very narrative form of Dracula and accounts for its shape and its inconsistencies.[24] On the one hand, Stoker writes a strenuously realist, apparently polyphonic text whose purpose is a vindication of the sexual politics and moral economy of his British masters. And yet he fills that narrative with dislocating dreams of the rape and subversion of those masters. Those dreams, half wish fulfilment and half nightmare, remain to disconcert and disturb readers a century later. In other words, what presents itself as a problem at the level of narrative structuring, a problem described by its first reviewer in the *Athenaeum*, is a problem whose roots lie in political contradictions that were unresolved in Stoker's mind and in the collective mind of many in Stoker's position.

Francis Ford Coppola's film *Bram Stoker's Dracula* was released in the States in late 1992 and in Britain in early 1993 and repositions Stoker's myth of the alien in terms appropriate to the late twentieth century. Columbia and its backers invested millions in this project and could not rely on anything as vague as the allegedly archetypal power of myth to guarantee their profits. A massive marketing effort was made to ensure that the film sold. The home video was released promptly in 1992. Then in 1993 there was a video about that video (called *The Making of Bram Stoker's Dracula*) and a video game (*Bram Stoker's Dracula: The Video Game*). All three products featured advertisements for the other two. There was a record released along with the film called 'Love Song for a Vampire', which played as the credits rolled and which was written and performed by Annie Lennox. Also in 1993 Pan published both Fred Soberhagen and James V. Hart's *Bram Stoker's Dracula: The Novel of the Film* and Coppola and Hart's *Bram Stoker's Dracula: The Film and the Legend*, presumably calculating that the confusion caused to readers by issuing two books with the same main title and the same co-author mattered less than the marketing need to echo the film's title. 'The world is poised on the brink of vampire fever' claimed a BBC press release but, as Elaine Showalter noted at the time, a vast budget was devoted to making sure the fever was infectious.[25]

Coppola himself became both beneficiary and victim of this phenomenon, a nice instance of Marx's point about people as both makers and objects of history. The journal he kept during the shooting of the film is at first full of high art references: the entry for 8 August 1991, for example, flows from Prokofiev to Eisenstein, from Cocteau to the Symbolists and surrealism. But a year later, on 15 August 1992, there is gloom about the demands of 'the professional film industry' and its money: 'you get the stars, you get everything else that you hate'. By the time the movie is released in the States he himself is only able to talk about the project in cash terms. On 19 November 1992 he writes: 'I knew that it would have to do at least seven or eight million dollars for it not to be a disgrace. Over ten would be really good.' Then the figures came through: '31½ million in the first weekend. It was a success and it saved my neck.'[26] Eat your heart out, Prokofiev.

Investment on this scale alone makes it inevitable that Coppola's *Dracula* would be made to address a wider audience than the more parochial concerns of earlier film versions of the story. A jumble of international stars was assembled for the filming in Culver City, California, to give the product global appeal. The result is that a Welsh Anthony Hopkins is made to struggle with the Irish Bram Stoker's idea of Van Helsing's Dutch accent as refracted through the film script of the American James V. Hart. Fellow Americans Winona Ryder and Keanu Reeves play the thoroughly British Harkers while the English Gary Oldman has a plucky stab at Dracula's Transylvanian vowels. Japanese money from Sony Pictures underpins the whole enterprise.

In short, Coppola's film repositions Dracula as boldly as his Oscar-winning 1979 movie *Apocalypse Now* had realigned Conrad's *Heart of Darkness*. His title, with its apparently authenticating inclusion of Stoker's name, is simply a device to ward off copyright problems with earlier films of the novel rather than an attempt to indicate any slavish following of the original text. His film sets out to replace Stoker's meanings, not to copy them, and once again we can find a short route to his new meanings if we look at the way the work begins.

The first shot is of a stone cross soon caught in swirls of smoke before smashing to pieces. Anthony Hopkins's voice-over informs the audience: 'The year, 1462. Constantinople had fallen. Moslem Turks swept into Europe ... threatening all Christendom. From Transylvania arose a Romanian knight, Dracule [*sic*].' Very briefly, we see Dracule kissing his wife Elizabeth before departing to secure an amazing victory over massive Turkish forces. But a false Turkish message informs Elizabeth of Dracule's death. She commits suicide and hence the church pronounces: 'She has taken her own life. Her soul cannot be saved.' The grieving Dracule renounces God and stabs a stone cross, drinking the blood that flows copiously from the gash opened in the stone by his sword. Subtitles then read: 'London, 1897. Four centuries later' and we reconnect approximately with Stoker's novel.

The project here is fairly straightforward. Stoker's text is being given a short new prelude before the opening credits whose clear aim is to make the Western viewer sympathise with Dracula as heroic outcast, a sympathy reinforced for the decoding viewer by the star system (the part is played by Gary Oldman). He is presented in terms that have only the vaguest relation to historical fact as a gallant defender of Christian civilisation against Islamic imperialism. In addition, his story is given irresistible echoes of Romeo and Juliet, the star-crossed lovers whose passion is aborted by a similarly false and suicide-inducing message.

There are elements in James V. Hart's early draft of this prologue that detract from the simple image of a valiant romantic. For instance, a voice-over describes Dracule as 'notorious throughout Eastern Europe for his bloodthirsty ways'. And then his own shouted battle order 'Impale the Sultan's wounded for all to see' provokes one of his own lieutenants to protest vainly: 'I beg you my Prince – do not do this. Haven't enough died this day?'[27] Both of these negative references are cut in the final filmed version of the screenplay, thus removing a potential source of damage to the initial projection of Dracula as a brave knight. The shooting of the battle scenes with the Turks in silhouette, as well as blanking out the gore, deliberately contributes further to a powerful initial impression of two-dimensional valour and comic-strip courage. As Gary Oldman pointed out, in a claim that says more about the film's ideological project than it does about the accuracy of his Biblical knowledge, his aim was to play Dracula not as a 'Devil' but as 'Raphael, a fallen angel, the angel that fell from grace'.[28]

We can understand the point of this direct, opening appeal for sympathy if we situate the film in the context of the early 1990s concern about an AIDS pandemic. Dracule's furious swallowing of the blood that streams across the screen at the start must strike any viewer as odd but would seem a particularly chilling act to an AIDS-aware audience.[29]

But, having hailed the AIDS issue, what does the director do with it? It is here that the project seems to me to lose its way. Coppola, in the year that he completed filming it, was centrally aware of the challenge of AIDS. In that summer of 1992 he was working on another film project called Cure about the search for a remedy for the HIV virus. He attended a conference on the subject that moved him deeply and in his journal for 23 July he noted:

> Now, after the conference in Amsterdam, I see the truth about this AIDS epidemic. People will never make love again without prophylactics ... People cannot be as promiscuous as their instincts; sex with a stranger can kill you. How sad for the future of love and romance![30]

But a nostalgic farewell to hedonism is not what Columbia Pictures was looking for, as Coppola noted in a rueful interview published as the film opened in London in January 1993:

> If I had written the script, I might have started it with Bram Stoker coming back from the doctor having been told he had syphilis, and the whole thing would be his nightmare. But part of being a good boy meant doing it with the script they [Columbia] liked.[31]

The script that Columbia liked was by James V. Hart who had none of Coppola's wistfulness for a vanishing world of friendly humping. Hart told television viewers on *The South Bank Show* in that same month that the key to the story for him was 'the incredible fear men have of unbridled female sexual energy'. Coppola then works with a script that ferociously tangles his own sympathy for AIDS victims with a frozen hatred of both sexuality in general and female sexuality in particular. A film riding on such heavy investment could not deal honestly with AIDS because it could not trade off an available consensus when none existed. In the end all it can do is raise the issue, gesture at it from a variety of generic directions – part Gothic horror, part comic-strip adventure, part Merchant/Ivory trip through Victorian London – but then settle for the easy solution: blame the women. Stoker's group of strait-laced gentlemen are faithfully reproduced and Dracula himself, as I have argued, is very sympathetically presented. But the film determinedly subverts Stoker's women. For example, in two early scenes that have no textual basis, Lucy and Mina are presented as giggling with hypocritical innocence at pornographic pictures and shortly afterwards Lucy addresses the naive American Quincey Morris with a series of salacious innuendoes apparently borrowed from the cutting room floor of a *Carry On* film.

Stoker himself offers enough additional material for a movie that plays off fear and hatred of women, most obviously in the scenes of sadistic piety surrounding the staking and decapitation of Lucy (for her own good of course) which the film lovingly reproduces. But my point is that to centre and embellish such material in the context of the AIDS panic is to lend an ugly boost to the forces of male chauvinism and Western Puritanism, dull brutes at the best of times but emerging with a newly potent nastiness after this treatment. Stoker's alien and terrifying other, born out of unresolved contradictions in his attitudes to Britain and British imperialism, is reborn in 1992 as a disconcertingly different and yet familiar figure. Columbia Pictures offers a new myth in which ancient fears of the instability and power of female sexuality erupt with fresh potency in the age of AIDS.

What I have sought to do in this chapter is best described by Marx in the eighth of his *Theses on Feuerbach*: 'All social life is essentially practical. All mysteries which lead theory to mysticism find their rational solution in human practice and the comprehension of this practice.'[32] By looking at and trying to comprehend one small area of cultural practice I want to float critical theory away from the higher shores of mysticism where it sometimes seems in danger of being permanently beached these days and instead use it as a craft which can carry us towards understanding. What emerges from an examination of this novel published in 1897 and remade as a significant film in 1992 is an apparently paradoxical sense that the prime ideological function of the horror genre is reassurance. Stoker's novel visited and, through his form of closure, calmed the fears that troubled his British middle-class readership.[33] Coppola's film hailed the anxieties that beset contemporary audiences, especially about AIDS, and then, in the classic move of ideology, offered fantastic or reactionary solutions in order to appease, control and reassure those audiences.

That is a simple but not inaccurate way of putting it. However, more needs to be said. It is for a start important to note that those cultural practices were, in their actual realisation, rendered paradoxical and contradictory. As we have seen, Stoker's project on behalf of the British he admired was undercut by his rebellious sympathy for the Ireland that gave him birth. The alien threat of Dracula is smashed, but in a process that torments and shatters his imperial destroyers. As a result, the British in the narrative are simultaneously revered and ravished, embraced and eviscerated, a ragingly complex construction that clearly has a mediated, continuing life in the Protestant politics of the island of Ireland and accounts in part for the undiminished momentum of the fable more than a century later. That internal conflict which we see in Stoker contrasts with the external conflict that seems to muddle the 1992 film, a conflict between Coppola's liberal instincts on sexual matters and the more straightfor-wardly conservative values that inform Hart's script and Columbia's investment.

Blurred meanings, fudged messages and confused signals are the hallmarks of the cinema because it is a highly collabora-tive medium with creative input from immensely varied directions. What emerges from such a massive matrix is inevitably neither Hollywood head-fixing nor bourgeois propaganda nor subversive insight nor radical agitprop but a fraught negotiation between these and many other forces as each makes its input into the final product, a final product, though, that always remains under the control of the studio and its dominant financial and ideological drives.

In Bram Stoker's novel Dracula is marked by his ability to assume different identities and inhabit other forms. He can bewilder his pursuers by shifting in a moment from Transylvanian count to howling wolf. The myth that he has fathered shows the same remarkable flexibility in the twentieth century. The wrong response to that diversity is Daniel Farson's traditionalist complaint about films that are not faithful to Stoker's original. After all, the first person to fail to be faithful to Stoker's original was Stoker himself when he lopped 25,000 words out of the text for Constable's abridged sixpenny edition, or earlier when he produced a stage version that the watching Henry Irving loudly described as 'Dreadful!' The power and appeal of myths lies not in their steady regard for allegedly unchanging aspects of the human psyche but rather in their endlessly demonstrated adaptability, their readiness to be shifted and shunted, reworked and recast to embody and soothe the anxieties and panics of the moment. As the beholders of those transformations, we in our turn need to be vigilant, aware and ready to do battle for those readings that enhance and extend the project of human liberation, alert and prepared to contest those inflexions that work to narrow the lives of men and women.[34]

Notes

1. *Guardian*, G2, 4 January 1994, p. 9.
2. Daniel Farson, *The Man Who Wrote Dracula: A Biography of Bram Stoker* (London: Michael Joseph, 1975), p. 168. 'Based', of course, is a loose term and other estimates are very different. Elaine Showalter, *Sexual Anarchy: Gender and Culture at the Fin-de-Siècle* (Harmondsworth: Penguin Books, 1991) notes 'over 133 full-length film versions' by 1980 (p. 182) while Leonard Wolf (ed.), *The Essential Dracula* (New York: Plume, 1993) finds 'more than two hundred' (p. viii).
3. Karl Marx, *The Eighteenth Brumaire of Louis Bonaparte* (New York: International, 1963), p. 15.

4. Christopher Frayling, 'Just a Kiss at Bedtime', *Guardian*, 14 November 1991; David Punter, *The Literature of Terror: A History of Gothic Fictions from 1765 to the Present Day* (London: Longman, 1980), p. 424; Phyllis A. Roth, *Bram Stoker* (Boston: Twayne, 1982), p. 87.

5. Clive Leatherdale, *Dracula: The Novel and the Legend* (London: Thorsons 1985), p. 11; Farson, *The Man Who Wrote Dracula*, p. 167.

6. For the middle-class readership of Victorian fiction, see Darko Suvin, 'The Social Addressees of Victorian Fiction', *Literature and History*, 8: 1 (Spring 1982), pp. 11–40. Early reviews of Dracula are conveniently summarised in Leatherdale, *Dracula*, p. 69.

7. A small sample of these voices includes Carol A. Senf, '*Dracula*: Stoker's Response to the New Woman', *Victorian Studies*, 26 (Autumn 1982), pp. 33–49; Robin Wood, 'Burying the Undead: The Use and Obsolescence of Count Dracula', *Mosaic*, 16: 1–2 (Winter–Spring 1983), pp. 175–87; Bram Dijkstra, *Idols of Perversity: Fantasies of Feminine Evil in Fin-de-Siècle Culture* (Oxford: Oxford University Press, 1986), pp. 341–8; Marjorie Howes, 'The Mediation of the Feminine: Bisexuality, Homoerotic Desire and Self-Expression in Bram Stoker's *Dracula*', *Texas Studies in Literature and Language*, 30: 1 (Spring 1988), pp. 104–19; Burton Hatlen, 'The Return of the Repressed/Oppressed in Bram Stoker's *Dracula*' in Margaret L. Carter (ed.), *Dracula: The Vampire and the Critics* (Ann Arbor: UMI Research Press, 1988), pp. 117–35; Christopher Craft, '"Kiss Me with Those Red Lips": Gender and Inversion in Bram Stoker's *Dracula*' in Carter (ed.), *Dracula*, pp. 167–94; Rosemary Jann, 'Saved by Science? The Mixed Messages of Stoker's *Dracula*', *Texas Studies in Literature and Language*, 31: 2 (Summer 1989), pp. 273–87; Malcolm Smith, '*Dracula* and the Victorian Frame of Mind', *Trivium*, 24 (1989), pp. 76–97; Sian Macfie, '"They Suck Us Dry": A Study of Late Nineteenth-Century Projections of Vampiric Women' in Philip Shaw and Peter Stockwell (eds), *Subjectivity and Literature from the Romantics to the Present Day* (London: Pinter, 1991), pp. 58–67; and Elaine Showalter, *Sexual Anarchy*, pp. 179-84. For some of the

    problems with this type of psycho-sexual reading of
    Dracula, see Stephen Arata, *Fictions of Loss in the Victorian
    Fin-de-Siècle* (Cambridge: Cambridge University Press,
    1996), pp. 111–14.

8. Bram Stoker, *Dracula*, ed. Maurice Hindle (Har-
    mondsworth: Penguin Books, 1993), p. 6.

9. Ibid., p. 7.

10. Bram Stoker, *Dracula's Guest* (Dingle: Brandon, 1990),
    p. 9.

11. Ibid., p. 23.

12. Ibid., p. 101.

13. Ibid., p. 155.

14. Details in this paragraph are from David Glover, *Vampires,
    Mummies and Liberals: Bram Stoker and the Politics of Popular
    Fiction* (London: Duke University Press, 1996), Barbara
    Belford, *Bram Stoker: A Biography of the Author of 'Dracula'*
    (London: Phoenix, 1997) and Peter Haining and Peter
    Tremayne, *The Un-Dead: The Legend of Bram Stoker and
    Dracula* (London: Constable, 1997). Recently, critics such
    as these have started to pay much more attention to the
    fact of Stoker's Irishness (though the conclusions they
    derive from that fact differ from those argued here). Even
    a text as recent as Declan Kiberd's wonderful *Inventing
    Ireland* (London: Jonathan Cape, 1995), a survey of Irish
    culture from Wilde to Friel, has only one brief reference
    to Stoker in its 719 pages.

15. See for example James B. Twitchell, *The Living Dead: A
    Study of the Vampire in Romantic Literature*, (Durham, NC:
    Duke University Press, 1981), p. 133; Wood, 'Burying the
    Undead', p. 178; and Jules Zanger, '"A Sympathetic
    Vibration": Dracula and the Jews', *English Literature in
    Transition*, 34: 1 (1991), p. 36.

16. Mikhail Bakhtin, *The Dialogic Imagination*, ed. Michael
    Holquist (Austin: University of Texas Press, 1981),
    pp. 366–71.

17. David Seed, 'The Narrative Method of *Dracula*' in Carter
    (ed.) *Dracula*, p. 199.

18. Franco Moretti, *Signs Taken for Wonders: Essays in the
    Sociology of Literary Forms* (London: NLB, 1983), p. 96;
    Chris Baldick, *In Frankenstein's Shadow: Myth, Monstrosity*

and Nineteenth-Century Writing (Oxford: Oxford University Press, 1987), pp. 147–8.

19. In a parallel way, Stephen Arata has argued that Stoker's ambivalent feelings about his English patron Irving are expressed in the construction of Dracula, many of whose details are derived from Irving and his appearance. See Arata, *Fictions of Loss*, p. 120.

20. Bram Stoker, *The Lair of the White Worm* (Dingle: Brandon, 1991), p. 155.

21. Bram Stoker, *Personal Reminiscences of Henry Irving* (London: Heinemann, 1906), Vol. 2, p. 31.

22. Ibid., Vol. 1, p. 251.

23. Ibid., Vol. 1, pp. 315–26. As Belford notes, this massive list finds no room for the name of Oscar Wilde, an old friend and frequent diner at the Lyceum. In June 1897, Wilde had only just emerged from Reading Gaol and his name was unmentionable in the polite circles *Personal Reminiscences* sought to entertain.

24. On these contradictions, see in particular Hatlen, 'Return of the Repressed/Oppressed', pp. 132–3, and Glover, *Vampires*, p. 152.

25. Elaine Showalter, 'Blood Sell', *Times Literary Supplement*, 8 January 1993, p. 14.

26. Francis Ford Coppola, 'Coppola Revealed', *Guardian*, G2, 23 March 1994, pp. 4–5.

27. James V. Hart, 'Dracula: The Untold Story', revised first draft of screen adaptation, 29 September 1990, pp. 1 and 2. Typescript in my possession.

28. Gary Oldman speaking to Melvyn Bragg on *The South Bank Show*, 24 January 1993.

29. The film was linked to AIDS by its earliest reviewers – see, for example, Jonathan Romney, 'At the Court of Coppola', *Guardian*, G2, 21 January 1993, p. 2. This has now become a standard reading of the film – see, for example, Jill Nelmes (ed.), *An Introduction to Film Studies* (London: Routledge, 1996), pp. 136 and 248.

30. Coppola, 'Coppola Revealed', p. 5.

31. Quoted in Romney, 'At the Court of Coppola', p. 3.

32. Loyd D. Easton and Kurt H. Guddat (eds), *Writings of the Young Marx on Philosophy and Society* (New York: Anchor Books, 1967), p. 402.
33. Similar views of the ideological function of Gothic fiction in general and *Dracula* in particular can be found in Punter, *The Literature of Terror*, pp. 421–3; Daniel Pick, '"Terrors of the Night": *Dracula* and Degeneration in the Late Nineteenth Century', *Critical Quarterly*, 30 (Winter 1988), pp. 71–87; Joseph Grixti, *Terrors of Uncertainty: The Cultural Contexts of Horror Fiction* (London: Routledge, 1989), pp. 8–14; Jeremy Tambling, *Narrative and Ideology* (Milton Keynes: Open University Press, 1991), p. 78; Arata, *Fictions of Loss*, p. 126.
34. This chapter is an updated, amalgamated and altered version of two papers originally given at the Culture and Colonialism conference at University College, Galway, in June 1995 and the Marxism 95 conference at the School of Oriental and African Studies, London, in July 1995. My thanks to participants at both conferences who commented helpfully on these early drafts of the present piece.

5

Another Time, Another Space: Modernity, Subjectivity, and *The Time Machine*

Jonathan Bignell

H.G. Wells's science fiction novels have long been attractive to film-makers. Film versions include *The Island of Dr Moreau* (Erle C. Kenton, 1932 (titled *The Island of Lost Souls*), Don Taylor, 1977, John Frankenheimer, 1996), *The Invisible Man* (James Whale, 1933, sequels Joe May, 1940, Ford Beebe, 1944), *Things to Come* (William Cameron Menzies, 1936), and *The War of the Worlds* (Byron Haskin, 1953). I want to focus here on Wells's short novel *The Time Machine*, first published in 1895, and the film adaptation directed by George Pal (1960).[1] *The Time Machine* does feature strange creatures, but not aliens in the usual science fiction sense. The central character, unnamed in the novel but called George Wells in the film, is a late nineteenth-century inventor who constructs a sled-like vehicle enabling him to travel into the future. In the year 802,701, the Time Traveller discovers two races of humanoids, the Eloi and the Morlocks. In the novel the frail and childlike Eloi are the passive and effete descendants of the elite of an advanced society, living in a sunlit paradise on the surface. The Morlocks are the ape-like cannibal descendants of the workers who operated the subterranean machines that kept this elite supplied with all its needs. This vision of the future counters the Victorian myth of progress, and explores the interdependence of workers and masters, perverted into the dependence of the Morlocks on the flesh of the Eloi who they formerly served. The Time Traveller realises that evolutionary development toward technical refinement and social order will lead to decadence (in the Eloi) and to savagery (in the Morlocks) at the same time.

In Pal's film version, a global war fought with nuclear weapons has exhausted the resources of this future society, and the remnants of the race have divided into those who continued to dwell on the irradiated surface (who became the Eloi) and those who stayed in underground shelters (and became the Morlocks). Clearly, the Cold War nuclear fears of 1960 have informed the future vision of Pal's film, just as anxieties around Darwinism and class conflict fuel the novel. The changes made to the narrative in the film version essentially involve the updating of the journey into the future so that the fears and fantasies of 1960 can be included.[2] Each version of *The Time Machine* explores future times which are by definition alien to the audience, but this alienness is necessarily consonant with familiar ideas.

My focus here is less on the alienness of the creatures in the future than on the alienness yet familiarity of the time travel experience and the futuristic settings of the story. The Time Traveller becomes a spectator who watches time move like a speeded-up film, and stops several times to explore the future scene. Like the cinema spectator, the Time Traveller sits on a red plush seat and watches a marvellous spectacle, and the journey into the future depends on a machine, a technological apparatus rather than magic or dream. The subjective experience being outlined in the novel is a subjectivity to be developed in cinema and in modern consumer culture in general, where technology transports the consumer to a virtual environment primarily experienced visually. Temporal mobility in *The Time Machine*, as in cinema, allows the subject to encounter what is alien, yet necessarily familiarises this as a consumable media experience. But time travel allows more than a cinematic visual spectacle. Since the hundreds of centuries traversed in the Time Traveller's fictional journey involve changes in buildings, people and even the geology of the landscape, the journey through time is in effect a tourist trip to alien spaces that he can leave his seat to explore. The Time Machine itself, as described in the novel and portrayed in Pal's film, looks like a sled with brass rails and over-decorated Victorian ornaments. It has a large revolving dish mounted vertically behind the inventor, and coloured lights and indicators on its control surface. The Time Machine is envisioned on an analogy with a machine for travelling in space rather than time, signalling the association between temporal movement and spatial movement.

Both the novel and the film are predicated on what Anne Friedberg has called a *'mobilized "virtual" gaze'*, a characteristic aspect of modernity developing through the nineteenth century into the twentieth, whereby movement in space and time is simulated by visual apparatuses of representation: 'The *virtual gaze* is not a direct perception but a *received* perception mediated through representation. I introduce this compound term in order to describe a gaze that travels in an imaginary *flânerie* through an imaginary elsewhere and an imaginary elsewhen.'[3] Wells's fictional Time Traveller experiences the future directly, but the reader of the story and the viewer of the film experience a mediated version of this, mediated through language in the novel, and through the visual and aural resources of cinema in the film. The reader or spectator becomes a *flâneur* or stroller, led on an exploratory journey through alien worlds. Friedberg continues: 'The cinema developed as an apparatus that combined the "mobile" with the "virtual". Hence, cinematic spectatorship changed, in unprecedented ways, the concepts of the *present* and the *real*.'[4] In both Wells's novel and Pal's film adaptation, travel in time is experienced predominantly as a visual experience. But one of the main attractions of the novel and the film is the ability to stop the headlong rush into the future, so that the Traveller can stop and stroll around in a realistically presented space. Time travel, like cinema, renders the moment virtual in order to allow a real-seeming experience of an alien space-time. Time travellers and cinema spectators are displaced from the reality of their own present and their own real location in order to be transported to 'an imaginary elsewhere and an imaginary elsewhen'.

The opening of Pal's film makes it clear that it is the cinema spectator who will be moved in virtual space and time and who will become the virtual subject of the time travel experience. It begins with a collection of brightly lit timepieces, appearing in chronological order of their invention, moving out of the black and dimensionless space of the screen towards the spectator. It is as if the spectator is travelling through space, plunging headlong into black emptiness with the cinema screen functioning as a window onto the journey. The final clock is London's Big Ben, tilted at an angle, as the hour is heard to strike. Lightning flashes and thunder crashes as the shot changes to a rapidly rising sun over which the film's title is superimposed. Then leaves and snow blow across a blue sky, succeeding each other rapidly as the seasons rush past. The first scene establishes the interior of the inventor's house, and the camera pans over a large collection of watches, mantel clocks and grandfather clocks, continuing the time motif and associating the spectator's own plunge through time with the interests of the central character. Already we can see that there is a slippage between the spectating subject in the cinema and the central time-travelling character. Furthermore, travel in time is parallel to travel in space, as the rushing forward movement past a series of clocks makes rather literally evident.

George Pal was drawn to Wells's story in part because it provided opportunities for state-of-the-art visual effects. His film version of *The Time Machine* uses many techniques including accelerated motion, reverse motion, pixellation, model shots and mattes to render the experience of time travel, and the future worlds the Traveller encounters, with as much verisimilitude as was possible in 1960. Pal was a specialist in these technologies of illusion. He began his career as a puppeteer making short advertising films in the late 1930s. In 1940 he went to Hollywood and moved on to adventure films where he specialised in trick effects, receiving an Academy Award in 1943 for his development of innovative methods and techniques. The films he worked on included *Destination Moon* (Irving Pichel, 1950), *When Worlds Collide* (Rudolph Maté, 1951), *The War of the Worlds*, *Tom Thumb* (1958, which he also directed) and *The Time Machine*. All of these films won Oscars for their special effects. Pal's special skill, then, was to realise the incredible, to make the alien and strange comprehensible according to visual conventions we can accept. In this respect he was part of a long tradition in cinema where, since the emergence of the medium, film had been used as a support for wondrous spectacles, where what was absent, novel, distant or unfamiliar became vividly present as part of an entertainment for the paying consumer.

Science fiction, historiography and archaeology, which all blossomed in the later decades of the nineteenth century, share an interest in time: representing a future moment, a documented moment in the past, or an arrested time which we can uncover and see. Time travel in literature in the work of Wells or Jules Verne appears at the same period as stories about lost civilisations in Conan Doyle's *The Lost World*, and novels by Bulwer Lytton and Butler. It is in this period that Roman sites in Britain, the pyramids and Mycenae were excavated, and Arthur Evans recreated parts of the Bronze Age city of Knossos in Crete so that tourists could walk around it. The common feature in these different aspects of culture is the refinement of techniques of representation which can make what is past, absent or fantastic into something which can be recreated, simulated and rendered virtually present for an individual subject. Similarly, the beginning of cinema is associated with nineteenth-century science's quest for knowledge of the physical world, with that period's obsession with memory, death and preservation, with fairground trick effects, magic and the supernatural, and with the possibilities of exploiting mechanical inventions for a mass consumer public. All of these aspects of the culture of modernity are signalled near the beginning of *The Time Machine*. The story is told mainly in flashback in both the novel and in Pal's film, as a dishevelled inventor appears late to meet his houseguests, and tells the story of his time travels. The first flashback returns us to the day when his guests were shown a model Time Machine vanishing, an experiment which all four of them believe may be a parlour trick, like the seances, magic lantern shows and short novelty films of the period. Like the spectators of the first films, the Time Traveller's audiences are thrown into doubt about the evidence of their own eyes. For them, the disappearance of the model Time Machine might be real, but more likely a trick, a simulation, a scientific demonstration or an optical illusion. *The Time Machine*, then, exploits the distinction between the virtual and the real, a distinction fundamental to the culture of modernity and to cinema.

Wells's novel was written amid a long-standing fascination with visually based representational devices in the late nineteenth century, exemplified by the dioramas, panoramas and other proto-cinematic devices of the period. Dioramas and panoramas were buildings where groups of spectators were presented with large back-lit illuminated images painted on semi-transparent screens, and used highly realistic painted backdrops and carefully arranged effects of perspective and depth of field to seem to place the spectator in a remote landscape, or at the occurrence of a famous past event. They offered the viewer a highly realistic visual environment, representing places to which the great majority of people could never go. These devices were enthralling because they transported the spectator to alien places and alien times by means of visual technologies and supporting special effects. What was there to be seen might be alien, a vision of another place and another time, but the whole spectacle depended on the spectator's familiarity with how to look, and on some familiarity with the cultural significance of what was represented. Effects of perspective, of the play of light and shade, were carefully calculated to be as real-seeming as possible, to allow the spectator to immerse himself or herself in the sense of 'being there' in the scene. Although the spectator would never have visited the great cathedral of Chartres, the eve of the Battle of Waterloo or the Swiss Alps, these places and events had already to be culturally established as significant and recognisable, so that there was a peculiar thrill in seeing them in all their grandeur. Like any consumer technology or media experience, the new, the alien, the surprising, had to be balanced with the expected, the familiar and the conventional.

In the novel and the film, time travel is a curious mixture of scientific experiment and fairground thrills. The experience of time travel gives the inventor in the novel 'a feeling exactly like that one has upon a switchback – of a helpless headlong motion!'[5] The Doctor in Pal's film version, one of the inventor's guests, suggests that the Time Machine is of no use or commercial value. Instead, he recommends that the inventor should do something to help Britain in the ongoing Boer War. The inventor is presented as a scientist who resists the military or commercial potential of his work, and his trip into the future seems to be an escape from war and commerce. As if escaping into the virtual world of the cinema, to a film in which he is both spectator and central character, the Time Traveller quits the time and space of his quotidian present. As Walter Benjamin wrote:

> Our taverns and our metropolitan streets, our railroad stations and our factories appeared to have locked us up hopelessly. Then came the film and burst this prison-world asunder by the dynamite of the tenth of a second, so that now, in the midst of its far-flung ruins and debris, we calmly and adventurously go travelling.[6]

Like the newly invented cinema, time travel frees the subject from the present and the real, to replace these with a virtual present and a virtual reality which is novel, exciting and technological. Like cinema technology, time travel seems to offer opportunities for science as well as tourism and commercial entertainment, yet the appeal of both Wells's story and of Pal's film is based on the pleasures of fantasy and speculation which they offer, rather than the exploration of the geometric and physical principles which each version refers to in order to ground time travel in scientific fact.

While early pioneers used film to explore the science of animal movement and to record contemporary life, entertainment rapidly became the most commercially successful use for the new technology. In 1894 the first Edison Kinetoscope parlour opened in New York, offering films of less than a minute, viewed by individual spectators who peeked into the Kinetoscope cabinets to see vaudeville performers and famous personalities. The film historian Terry Ramsaye wrote to Wells in 1924 asking whether the idea for *The Time Machine* was born from Wells's experience of the Edison Kinetoscope.[7] Wells replied that he did not remember any connection between early motion pictures and the writing of the story, though the description of the Time Traveller's first jaunt into the future is highly suggestive of cinema. The Time Traveller is in his laboratory, and catches sight of his housekeeper just before he accelerates forward in time:

Mrs. Watchett came in and walked, apparently without seeing me, towards the garden door. I suppose it took her a minute or so to traverse the place, but to me she seemed to shoot across the room like a rocket. I pressed the lever to its extreme position. The night came like the turning out of a lamp, and in another moment came to-morrow. The laboratory grew faint and hazy, then fainter and ever fainter. To-morrow night came black, then day again, night again, day again, faster and faster still.[8]

The experience is entirely visual and places the Time Traveller in the role of film-maker (controlling the machine) and spectator at the same time. As he speeds forward, the flickering motion of a film projector is suggested in the rapid alternation of day and night. The Kinetoscope allowed the novelty of seeing simple action speeded up or reversed, which was one of the most entertaining aspects of early films for their spectators. Films showed the acceleration of mechanical or natural processes (like the growth of plants), and this is mirrored when the Time Traveller sees 'great and splendid architecture rising about me, more massive than any buildings of our own time, and yet, as it seemed, built of glimmer and mist. I saw a richer green flow up the hillside, and remain there without any wintry intermission.'[9] When the Time Traveller returns to his original time, he sees accelerated reverse motion:

I think I have told you that when I set out, before my velocity became very high, Mrs. Watchett had walked across the room, travelling, as it seemed to me, like a rocket. As I returned, I passed again across that minute when she traversed the laboratory. But now every motion appeared to be the exact inversion of her previous ones. The door at the lower end opened, and she glided quietly up the laboratory, back foremost, and disappeared behind the door by which she had previously entered.[10]

What both time travel and cinema can do is to make the familiar appear unfamiliar by changing the manner of its perception. What is rapid can be slowed down, what moves slowly can be speeded up, and forward motion can be reversed.

Time travel and cinema seem to show the spectator the workings of the laws of nature, granting him or her a special perception, which makes the ordinary marvellous and strange.

In Pal's film, the first journey through time uses various cinematic trick effects, and the laboratory has a large glazed wall which enables it to function like a cinema screen, through which the inventor seated at the machine can see a panorama of the changing world outside. Special effects include fast motion shots of the sun and clouds moving across the sky, a snail speeding across the floor, shadow and light flitting across the inventor and the machine, and people moving rapidly in the street across from the laboratory. While the sequence is anchored through shot-reverse shots to George's point of view, many of the fast motion sequences are not from his spatial position, and function to make us share George's wonder and disorientation (noted in the voice-over narration) as he makes this short hop into the future. Time travel and cinema place the spectator in a privileged position, able to see movement in a way alien to normal experience. Because the Time Traveller is moving so rapidly through time, the people he sees cannot see him, and events unfold as if he were not present. One of the components of cinematic pleasure explored by Christian Metz[11] and other film theorists is exactly this transcendent vision, where the cinema spectator seems to master and control what is seen on the screen, while being excluded from the action and removed from responsibility for it. The Time Traveller at this point, and the cinema spectator, are both apparent masters of vision, and also voyeurs of a world which they cannot enter.

In 1895 the Lumière brothers showed the first publicly projected films in Paris, exhibited at the Empire Music Hall in London in 1896. Also in 1895, the year *The Time Machine* was published, Robert Paul, a scientific instrument-maker from London who had copied and improved the Kinetoscope, designed a motion picture camera with his collaborator the photographer Birt Acres. By 1896 Robert Paul was showing his own films at Olympia in London and the Alhambra music hall, and had made the first British fiction film, *The Soldier's Courtship*. Ramsaye reports that Robert Paul read *The Time Machine* soon after its publication, and it gave him an idea for a new way to use the film medium.[12] Paul wrote to Wells, who visited him at his London studio. After the meeting with Wells, Paul entered patent application no. 19984, dated 24 October 1895, for 'A Novel Form of Exhibition or Entertainment, Means for Presenting the Same'.[13] It begins:

> My invention consists of a novel form of exhibition whereby the spectators have presented to their view scenes which are supposed to occur in the future or the past, while they are given the sensation of voyaging upon a machine through time.[14]

Paul's invention was never built, due to lack of funds, and belonged among a rash of inventions at the turn of the century which were combinations of film with diorama-like attractions or fairground magic effects. In 1904, for instance, at the St Louis Exhibition, George C. Hale presented Hale's Tours, where travelogue films were shown to spectators seated in a railway carriage, with train sound effects and a wobbling floor to simulate movement. The similarities between the descriptions of time travel in Wells's novel and the experience of cinema seem to have triggered Paul's idea for a virtual time travel attraction exploiting aspects of several recently invented technologies.

The mechanism was to be a 'platform, or platforms' which could contain a group of spectators enclosed on three sides, facing a screen on which 'views' were to be projected. The platform would be moved by cranks to produce 'a gentle rocking motion'.[15] While the platform was moving, fans would blow air over the spectators, simulating the effect of motion, or the fans could be visibly attached to the platform as if they were a means of propulsion.

> After the starting of the mechanism, and a suitable period having elapsed, representing, say, a certain number of centuries, during which the platforms may be in darkness, or in alternations of darkness and dim light, the mechanism may be slowed and a pause made at a given epoch, on which the scene upon the screen will gradually come into

view of the spectators, increasing in size and distinctness from a small vista, until the figures, etc., may appear lifelike if desired.[16]

Time travel would be simulated, as in Wells's novel, by a motion not unlike a fairground ride, and would involve passages from darkness to light reminiscent of Wells's description. It was important that the scene should be 'realistic', showing a 'hypothetical landscape, containing also the representations of the inanimate objects in the scene', and would use slides showing moving objects like a balloon which could 'traverse the scene'.[17] There would also be 'slides or films, representing in successive instantaneous photographs, after the manner of the kinetoscope, the living persons or creatures in their natural motions'.[18] To produce dissolves and to enlarge or reduce the picture area, the projectors would be mounted on moveable tracks, which could bring them closer to or further from the screen. Paul's invention reproduces Wells's fictional time travel experience quite closely: putting the spectator into a conveyance like a switchback car, so that travel in time felt not unlike travel in space, and presenting the journey through time as a movement through light and darkness where the spectator stops to see a future epoch in the form of a film. While the alienness of the experience is what is attractive, it resembles familiar experiences like a fairground ride and a film show.

In some ways, Paul's invention looks forward to the experience of watching Pal's 1960 film. Pal's film can offer a modern cinematic experience, where trick effects, synchronous sound and music, and the use of cuts and camera movement have been developed to encourage the spectator's identification with the action, a sense of verisimilitude and dramatic pacing. Despite the futuristic settings of the film, and the alienness of the creatures in the future (especially the blue-skinned, shaggy-haired and sharp-toothed Morlocks), by 1960 cinema was calculated to produce an impression of reality. Paul's invention drew on the familiar technology of nineteenth-century amusement parks, such as the movement of the car and the blowing of air over the spectators, to produce similar effects. Following the practice at dioramas and panoramas, Paul also planned to use built sets which the spectators could physically explore:

> In order to increase the realistic effect I may arrange that after a number of scenes from a hypothetical future have been presented to the spectators, they may be allowed to step from the platforms, and be conducted through grounds or buildings arranged to represent exactly one of the epochs through which the spectator is supposed to be travelling.[19]

Here physical movement and temporal movement appear together, and the spectating subject literally becomes a *flâneur* or stroller, on a tourist trip, complete with guide, through a three-dimensional simulation of the future. In Wells's novel and in Pal's film this experience has to be mediated through the spectator's identification with the Time Traveller himself, who narrates his journeys and describes his wonderment at what he sees, and whose point of view in the film is aligned with the camera as he enters buildings and explores new landscapes. In *The Time Machine* the Time Traveller is not only a voyeur but also a tourist having adventures in future locations, and Paul's invention clearly aimed to replicate this kind of experience.

In Pal's film the inventor stops to look around in 1917, 1940 and 1966. These interludes give the film the chance to create street scenes reminiscent of one of Robert Paul's future environments. The immediate space around the Time Traveller is a dressed set in each case, using glass shots for background, and different cars, costumes and shopfronts to establish location in time. In 1940 Pal departs from the Time Traveller's point of view and uses stock shots of blazing fighter planes, and a diorama model of London in the Blitz, but then from the Time Traveller's point of view the spectator witnesses post-war reconstruction. New concrete buildings rise and cranes and scaffolding grow up at high speed accompanied by jaunty music on the soundtrack. Accelerated motion is intended to be comic here, just as it was when the projector's ability to change the speed of natural movement was realised at the turn of the century. So far, the film has represented the known past in 1960, aiming for visual verisimilitude and focusing thematically on the immediate effects of war. In 1966, the projected future from the perspective of 1960 is like a sunny American suburb. The inventor's house (destroyed by a wartime bomb) has been replaced by a park. The local shop, which had become a department store by 1917, is now a glass and concrete shopping mall, and shiny American cars are in the street. The film's thematic emphasis on the effects of war continues as extras rush past and an air-raid siren sounds. As well as continuing the precise simulation of a realistic location, the film presents the future by extrapolation from a relatively pessimistic vision of humankind's folly. This virtual future environment is alien but familiar, all too obviously determined by a 1960 anxiety (but also shared by Wells in the 1895 novel) that the future will be the same as the present, only more so. The 1966 scene ends as an atomic blast devastates the street, volcanoes erupt, seemingly the earth's vengeance against humankind's misuse of atomic power, and lava streams shunt burned-out cars across the set.

The Time Traveller speeds forward to a landscape seen first in a wide establishing shot featuring a futuristic domed hall and tower falling into decay. Like Robert Paul's walk-through simulations of the future, the settings are 'realistic' in terms of visible detail, dimension, props and set dressing. In 802,701 the buildings and sets in Pal's film draw on an eclectic mix of forms familiar to the audience of 1960. The domed pavilions and towers are reminiscent of the structures built for Disneyland (which opened in 1955), the 1951 Festival of Britain, and other realised versions of the future built for the tourist visitor of the period. Settings are to some extent matched with contemporary preconceptions of the relation between architectural form and function, so that the dome in which decayed books and museum exhibits are found has the wide steps and frontage of a European or American palace of culture. The dark caverns inhabited by the cannibal Morlocks contain the heavy-industrial machines of a dank nineteenth-century factory, while the Morlocks' gruesome deserted dining area, littered with the bones and skulls of their Eloi prey, seems like a reconstruction of an archaeological site. The costumes of the sylvan and vegetarian Eloi are toga-like, and they are most often seen in a wooded and verdant setting like an idealised recreation of the civilisation of ancient Greece. Pal's version of the future is not visualised as a consistent environment. It is neither solely utopian nor dystopian in terms of the signification of elements of *mise en scène*, but draws on the cultural currency of signs in the physical environment which were in circulation in the period when the film was made. This virtual future is necessarily unlike the present the spectator knows, but far from alien because of the use of a bricolage of elements with familiar connotations and resonances.

Cinema in general, as the film theorist Jean-Louis Baudry argued, proceeds from a 'wish to construct a simulation machine capable of offering the subject perceptions which are really representations mistaken for perceptions'.[20] As theories of spectatorship have shown, the principle of cinema and other audio-visual technologies is to offer what is recognisable and familiar, balanced against the pleasures of the new, the alien, of what cannot be seen or experienced in quotidian reality. The spectator is moved through represented space and time, offered an imaginary spatial and temporary mobility. The case of *The Time Machine*, novel and film, provides a strikingly literal illustration of the principles of pleasure in representation, which cinema became focused on from a very early period in its development. A brief consideration of Paul's time travel spectacle links Wells's novel with cinema historically, showing that the novel was read, at least by someone who knew of the technical possibilities of the new medium, as a proto-cinematic experience. At the same time, as a science fiction story, *The Time Machine* reminds us that science fiction is especially significant in an examination of the subjectivity of modernity. Works in this genre often focus on spatial and temporal mobility and on the realisation of imaginary alien scenarios. The principle of science fiction is the simulation of an other world which is both alien yet representable through the conventions, competencies and technologies we already know. In 1902 in France, only a few years after Wells's novel was published and Paul had entered his patent for a time travel entertainment, the first science fiction film, *A Trip to the Moon*, was first shown. It portrayed a journey through space by means of a gigantic projectile to an alien world where strange creatures are encountered, and used theatrical sets, backdrops and trick effects drawing on the capabilities of the film camera. The film's director, Georges Méliès, had formerly made his career as a stage magician. Just a few years after Paul's idea for a time travel attraction, movement in time and space were simulated on the cinema screen, rather than by elaborate combinations of film, static images, built sets, viewing platforms and tour guides. The modern notions of travel in space and time, which Wells's novel narrated in such visual form, began to become the stock in trade of film as commercial entertainment for the individual consumer, enjoying a mobile gaze but sitting still in the auditorium. The subject in modernity, strolling either literally or by means of a mobile gaze, through a virtual reality associated with commodity consumption and mass enter-tainment, is both necessary to and furthered by the pleasures of cinema, time travel, science fiction and tourism.

Notes

1. Earlier and shorter versions of *The Time Machine* were 'The Chronic Argonauts', serialised in the *Science Schools Journal*, April to June 1888, and an uncredited and unfinished serial 'The Time Machine', March to June 1894 in the *National Observer*. In January to May 1895 the *New Review* published a serial 'The Time Machine' similar to the first book editions published in 1895 by Heinemann, London, and Henry Holt & Co., New York. The 1960 film *The Time Machine* was directed by George Pal, with a screenplay by David Duncan, produced by MGM/Galaxy, and stars Rod Taylor and Yvette Mimieux. Other versions of Wells's story on film and television include a faithful rendition on BBC television adapted and directed by Robert Barr (screened 25 January 1949, revised and repeated 21 February 1949), a Canadian film version directed by Terence McCarthy in 1973, and an American

1978 TV movie adaptation directed by Henning Schellerup.

2. There is insufficient space here to discuss the many differences between the novel and the film. For example, the endings are very different: in the novel, the Time Traveller journeys to a time when the earth is about to become lifeless, and, depressed, he returns to collect materials for gathering specimens from the future as evidence of his travels. In the film, he falls in love with Weena, an Eloi woman, and after returning briefly to his own time he sets off again to find her.

3. Anne Friedberg, *Window Shopping: Cinema and the Postmodern* (Berkeley, CA: University of California Press, 1993), pp. 2–3.

4. Ibid.

5. H.G. Wells, *The Time Machine*, in Harry M. Geduld (ed.), *The Definitive Time Machine: A Critical Edition of H.G. Wells's Scientific Romance with Introduction and Notes* (Bloomington and Indianapolis: Indiana University Press, 1987), p. 42. Geduld uses the text of Volume 1 of the Atlantic edition of Wells's work, H.G. Wells, *The Time Machine, The Wonderful Visit and Other Stories* (New York: Charles Scribner & Sons, 1924).

6. Walter Benjamin, 'The Work of Art in the Age of Mechanical Reproduction' in *Illuminations*, trans. Harry Zorn (New York: Schocken Books, 1969), p. 316.

7. Terry Ramsaye, 'Robert Paul and *The Time Machine*' from T. Ramsaye, *A Million and One Nights* (New York: Simon & Schuster, 1926), reprinted in Geduld, *The Definitive Time Machine*, p. 196.

8. Wells, *Time Machine*, pp. 41–2.

9. Ibid., p. 43.

10. Ibid., p. 87.

11. Christian Metz, *The Imaginary Signifier: Psychoanalysis and the Cinema* (Bloomington: Indiana University Press, 1982).

12. See Ramsaye 'Robert Paul and *The Time Machine*', p. 196.

13. The patent application is reprinted in full in Geduld, *The Definitive Time Machine*, pp. 198–9.

14. Ibid., p. 198.

15. Ibid.
16. Ibid.
17. Ibid.
18. Ibid.
19. Ibid., p. 199.
20. Jean-Louis Baudry, 'The Apparatus: Metapsychological Approaches to the Impression of Reality in Cinema' in P. Rosen (ed.), *Narrative, Apparatus, Ideology* (New York: Columbia University Press, 1986), p. 315.

6

'The Martians Are Coming!': Civilisation v. Invasion in *The War of the Worlds* and *Mars Attacks!*

Liz Hedgecock

> ... it is through learning to relate to the alien that man has learned to study himself.[1]

H.G. Wells's novel *The War of the Worlds* (1898) and Tim Burton's film *Mars Attacks!* (1996) are respectively the first and the latest versions of the Martian-invasion theme. I wish to explore how the impact of Martian invasion affects earth civilisation in these texts, with regard to the generic and media-based differences in their presentation of the motif, and their opposing positions in science fiction history, which divide them more than any differences in genre. Specifically, I wish to prove that much of the threat which Wells and Burton depict is not from the invasion of the Martians, but from the invasion and dominance of a mutated human civilisation. Wells expresses this explicitly by introducing evolutionary and imperialist themes, while Burton presents the demise of a society dependent on mass media. Both texts champion the individual over the collective, and mourn the loss of individual space. They also express the concept of invasion in their form as well as their content.

Science fiction is a genre which still experiences a film/fiction divide. The earliest books on science fiction film, such as John Baxter's *Science Fiction in the Cinema, 1895–1970* (1970), treat film as inferior to fiction, almost by definition. Richard Hodgens, writing in 1959, baldly states that 'H.G. Wells's *War of the Worlds* is a good novel, and difficult to ruin',[2] implying that if film adaptations manage to avoid mutilating the original texts beyond recognition, that is through the merit of the original rather than the film.

This standpoint is so widespread in early science fiction criticism that all critics who disagree are forced to use up space defending their view against the implicit one, often ingeniously. Susan Sontag attempts to overcome the controversy by treating science fiction film as entirely separate:

> while novel and film may share the same plot, the fundamental difference between the resources of the novel and the film makes them quite dissimilar ... Science films are not about science. They are about disaster, which is one of the oldest subjects of art.[3]

While Sontag's points are valid, she seems to want science fiction film to be an age-old establishment genre, a throwback fitting seamlessly into the artistic tradition. Brooks Landon, writing in 1992, is still on the defensive, equalising the two genres by burdening both with clumsy names, 'science fiction literature' and 'science fiction film', and this seems symbolic of the weighing down of all science fiction in the attempt to free some of it from its bad press. As President Dale says cheesily to the head Martian in *Mars Attacks!*, 'Why can't we just *get along*?' Sometimes, inevitably, the two genres use different languages, but often they are closely related and even turn out to be saying the same thing, namely that civilised humankind and invading aliens may not be as different as they (or we) think. Indeed, like the pigs and the men in George Orwell's *Animal Farm* (1945), it may become impossible to tell them apart.

Significantly, both Wells and Burton emphasise the potential rather than the actual humanity of the Martians – both texts deal primarily with what could be rather than what is. When Wells describes the physiological nature of the Martians, which appears very unlike ours, he remarks that they probably descended from beings like ourselves, the emotional side of their natures disappearing as their brain and hands evolved 'at the expense of the body'.[4] The obvious implication, which is left for the reader to infer, is that under the pressures of evolution humans may also develop into Martian-like creatures. But at least the Martians are driven by the necessity of escaping a dying planet, unlike the Victorians staking their claims in search of trade: indeed, Wells's Martians are in some respects more humane than humans, in that their preferred method of extinction, the Heat-Ray, is comparatively quick and painless.

Burton's Martians enjoy a kind of diminutive humanity; they manage to combine actually being the little green men the viewer expects with appearing distinctly humanoid. They show a lively interest in human popular culture, watching television and reading *Playboy*. However, they parody and distort it: *Playboy*, in an unspecified manner, gives the Martians the idea to swap the heads of Nathalie Lake and her dog Poppy. In many ways the Martians are childlike and mass-produced, like children with toys and like the toys themselves. The Martian soldiers are clamped into the two halves of their suits like toy soldiers on a production line, and their red and blue guns are identical to the arcade toys for which Cedric and Neville Williams play truant. The effectiveness of their weapons and strategies makes this arrested development dangerous. The Martian 'girl' who infiltrates the White House is a sex object exaggerated to almost grotesque proportions, with her improbable curves, big hair and mechanically sinuous walk, but she gets in. The Martians understand the concept of sexuality, but are immune to the sexual urge and no female Martians are ever seen, if indeed they exist.

In this respect Burton's and Wells's Martians are identical. Wells comments: 'wonderful as it seems in a sexual world, the Martians were absolutely without sex, and therefore without any of the tumultuous emotions that arise from that difference among men'.[5] Zoe Sofia makes a valuable point regarding this lack:

The suppression or absence of normal heterosexual intercourse, female gestation, and childbirth is a much stronger and more widespread marker of the science-fiction genre than the icons we usually think of, such as displacement in space and time, high technology, scientific extrapolation, and so forth.[6]

As if to emphasise this difference, *Mars Attacks!* is full of human couples – President and Mrs Dale, Art and Barbara Land, the Norrises, Billy Glenn and Sharona, Byron and Louise Williams, Nathalie Lake and Jason Stone, Nathalie and Donald Kessler, and finally Richie Norris and Taffy Dale. Regardless of the success of these partnerships, throughout the film characters are impelled by the Martian pursuit to pursue each other.

Taffy's enquiry whether Richie has a girlfriend suggests a Darwinian selection of a suitable partner. Richie's credentials are impeccable, since he is a survivor who has almost single-handedly eliminated the Martians. Taffy takes the phrase 'survival of the fittest' literally, but 'the fittest' in the world of the film is a category with an unexpected membership. Grandma Norris, good but frail and clearly wandering in her mind, survives, while the aggressive Billy Glenn lasts about ten minutes against the Martians. New Age alcoholic Barbara Land makes it, while dippy TV presenter Nathalie Lake doesn't (though she gets the best ending, dying as her disembodied head kisses Donald Kessler's and their flying saucer sinks beneath the waves).

The War of the Worlds presents a similarly skewed version of evolutionary theory. This owes a great deal to its historical context. The Martians' exodus from their dying planet parallels Britain's anxious expansion into new territories; expansion proves survival, which proves a fit nation. Significantly, Winfried Baumgart cites social Darwinism, which projects evolutionary ideas onto the future development of humankind, as both 'an impulse to imperialism and its justification'.[7] Elie Halévy explicitly relates exhaustion and expansion:

> England felt an increasingly powerful conviction that her vitality was less than that of certain other nations, and that if she was progressing, her rate of progress was less rapid than theirs – that is to say, if not absolutely, at least relatively to her rivals, she was declining. It was this loss of confidence which explains the far-reaching change in her foreign policy.[8]

Baumgart notes that 'during the first half of the nineteenth century people in Britain were already using the theory of evolution in order to explain and justify the unrivalled position that Britain had occupied in the world by then'. The fact that 'war was regarded as a mechanism of evolution',[9] and that social Darwinism justified and explained races' inability to survive as an evolutionary failure, would seem to suggest a very diseased outlook indeed in the *fin-de-siècle* mind. But much of social Darwinism's charm came from its goal of progress and continued development in human evolution, not unlike that of socialism in its aims, though different in its perspective.[10] For Wells, scientist, socialist, prophet and ameliorist, this tempting brew of qualities must have proved very difficult to resist.

The War of the Worlds is, in part, an allegory of colonialism gone mad. Between 1880 and 1898 Britain annexed Papua, Upper Burma and Zululand and established protectorates in Bechuanaland, Matabeleland, Nyasaland, Uganda, British East Africa and the Northern Territories.[11] Whatever the benefits for trade, the list sounds suspiciously like an attempt to spread as much pink over the world map as possible, a way to try and reassure the nation of its quality by increasing its quantity. Wells refers early in the novel to the dangers of the human impulse to colonise:

> we must remember what ruthless and utter destruction our own species has wrought, not only upon animals, such as the vanished bison and the dodo, but upon its own inferior races. The Tasmanians, in spite of their human likeness, were entirely swept out of existence in a war of extermination waged by European immigrants, in the space of fifty years.[12]

This passage reveals Wells's own ambivalence towards the British 'invasion' of territories. While the narrator shows his dislike for the 'ruthless and utter destruction' which 'our own species' has wrought, the characterisation of the Tasmanians as one of the 'inferior races' implies that the Tasmanians belong to a different species, that, lumped together with the animals, they are only marginally 'better' than animals themselves. A probably coincidental but suggestive feature in Wells's choice of Mars as aggressor is that Mars itself was colonised. When Mars was mapped by R.A. Proctor in 1867 its features were named for past and present astronomers. However, when Schiaparelli produced a superseding map in 1877 he renamed and therefore 'recolonised' everything, substituting classical names for personal ones: Herschel II. Strait became Sinus Sabaeus.[13]

In the novel Wells and the narrator are fundamentally sympathetic towards progress, often regardless of humanity. The narrator, who resembles Wells in many external details, is on the side of the Martians. Patrick Parrinder considers that '[o]ne of the great paradoxes of *The War of the Worlds* is that ... it is the Martians, rather than men, who finally emerge as romantic heroes'.[14] The narrator acts as a distanced, even alien reporter throughout: 'By ten o'clock the police organisation, and by midday even the railway organisations, were losing coherency, losing shape and efficiency, guttering, softening, running at last in that swift liquefaction of the social body.'[15] The word 'guttering' suggests the image of a candle burning and melting down, of time running out and light disappearing, of a world in darkness, without form and void, and there is a latent excitement in watching this destruction. The repeated images of melting evoke human organisation disintegrating into alien slime.

Several times the narrator is miraculously saved: 'Had that death swept through a full circle, it must inevitably have slain me in my surprise. But it passed and spared me, and left the night about me suddenly dark and unfamiliar.'[16] The narrator is, somehow, outside the realm of death, impervious to and thus kin to the Martians. He is one of the chosen few who have the strength to outwit the Martians; most of these seem to be related to the narrator or to his wife, suggesting the underlying doctrine of the survival of the fittest. The narrator presents the majority of people he meets, who are clearly Martian fodder, with something between pity and contempt, even in the abstract: 'Never before had I seen houses burning without the accompaniment of an obstructive crowd.'[17] One of the most wonderful sights for him is London empty and desolate: 'Those who have only seen London veiled in her sombre robes of smoke can scarcely imagine the naked clearness and beauty of the silent wilderness of houses.'[18]

Bernard Bergonzi states that *The War of the Worlds* embodies the *fin du globe* myth of the dissolution of the social order in a typically *fin-de-siècle* manner.[19] Yet the novel is more specific and thoughtful than this suggests. The narrator finally sees the Martian invasion as beneficial, stating that:

> it has robbed us of that serene confidence in the future which is the most fruitful source of decadence, the gifts to human science it has brought are enormous, and it has done much to promote the conception of the commonweal of mankind.[20]

The narrator sees the sort of civilisation displayed by the curate, his perpetual mixture of prayer, desperation, despair and disgust, as useless and harmful. For a time he is captivated by the uncivilised, social Darwinist utopia of the artilleryman, which proposes to do without the furbelows of civilisation,[21] but he rejects it when he realises that the artilleryman's plans, however practical, are so many castles in the air, and that his main objective is to revenge himself on anyone more fortunate than he is. Anne B. Simpson argues that the narrator and the artilleryman are very similar, and that the narrator leaves only because of 'the Other's failure to act out the narrator's desires'.[22] Another reason for the narrator's departure is that in his inaction the artilleryman has proved himself degenerate, unfit to survive, and thus proved his theories worthless.

Under the Martian threat the narrator's character itself degenerates. He only recovers his old self fully when he is reunited with his wife at the end, when he has something to live for other than simply living. In this instance humankind has survived, but it is shown as a very narrow escape. The Martians, who have simultaneously evolved and degenerated, are killed by their intolerance to earthly bacteria – an extremely ambivalent end, suggesting that evolution is degeneration. A recurrent image in *The War of the Worlds* is that of men or Martians forming a crescent shape, in defence or attack. This suggests a crescent moon; but the reader never finds out whether that moon is waxing or waning, growing to fullness or shrinking to nothing. It seems an appropriately ambiguous metaphor for the novel's evolution/degeneration debate.

Mars Attacks! features in an article by Jonathan Romney in the *Guardian* as one of a series of digital films which produce a controlled apocalypse. Romney sees the digital image as persuasive yet unable finally to affect its audience, and links the prevalence of apocalypse situations to a possible death of cinema. It is certainly true that the special effects in the film, from the Martians themselves to the destruction of national monuments, are so convincing as to seem almost normal. Romney also comments: 'We tend to think of Hollywood as being fixated on the past, in its tendency to thrive on sequels and remakes. But Hollywood in the late 1990s is addicted to the future, to technologies of novelty.'[23] This is a massive generalisation, but an interesting one when applied to Wells's novel and Burton's film. Both are simultaneously prospective and retrospective. Both draw on and make use of a variety of influences. Wells's novel is told retrospectively, but is set in the near future and is an allegory referring to the present. Burton's film uses the latest technology but has a deliberate 'retro' look. As for the concept of film at the end of the twentieth century producing controlled apocalypse, *The War of the Worlds* presents a controlled *fin-de-siècle* explosion in its own right, suggesting the phenomenon as a repetition enhanced by superior technology.

Wells portrays humankind as evolved or civilised to a point where people either cannot comprehend or cannot cope with danger. The warnings of Ogilvy the astronomer are disregarded because he is hatless. Burton presents a world where the majority of people experience vicariously, passively, and function collectively rather than as individuals, like the herd of stampeding cattle in the opening sequence of *Mars Attacks!*[24] The spread of technology is presented as being partly responsible for this change, and is regarded ambivalently in both works – paradoxically, since Wells is so interested in progress and Burton uses the latest technology to bring his imaginings to life. A possible early source for Wells's attitude is given in Norman and Jeanne MacKenzie's biography:

Bromley itself had been invaded. The second railway station, Bromley North, was built when Wells was eleven, and the new line quickly turned the village into a London suburb populated by white-collar commuters ... The jerry-built houses for clerks and working-men were run up along dead-end roads.[25]

This account is clearly touched with nostalgia, in that it relates more closely to *The War of the Worlds*, which is set in an idyllic Surrey about which the narrator is pointedly elegiac. This lyricism, though, includes the railway: 'My wife pointed out to me the brightness of the red, green and yellow signal lights hanging in a framework against the sky. It seemed so safe and tranquil.'[26] The once dreaded interloper has become an accepted part of life, but its lights still seem alien to the landscape, perhaps intended as a warning of things to come. The narrator is also trying to master a new technology in the form of the bicycle,[27] while Wells was cycling round Surrey to find appropriate locations and details for the novel.[28] This individual technology, though, seems to meet with approval. Groups, even such harmless and well-meaning ones as the deputation, tend to meet with disaster, while the lone artilleryman is approved of until it becomes clear that he cannot act alone. The narrator may have spoken of 'the commonweal of mankind',[29] but this abstract collective is only evoked once the danger has passed. Mass media, in the form of newspapers, is shown both as useless – in an emergency it cannot provide news – and yet as proof that the nation is not lost entirely.

Mars Attacks!, similarly, disapproves of collectives. Groups which are aware of their group status, such as Congress, the President's publicity machine, the army, or the spectators at Puhrump, are swiftly despatched. Individuals, or groups that form accidentally, like the odd assembly of Byron Williams, Tom Jones, Barbara Land and Cindy, survive. There are few 'normal' enclosed interiors – locations switch between the Norrises' trailer, the White House, where people are always being shown round, the casino, and various large purpose-built laboratory and conference spaces. Louise Williams's apartment is particularly odd, in that most of the action in it takes place in a turret room which is almost fully windowed. The final shot of the house shows it with the side blown off, exposing it in cross-section. These peculiar living spaces suggest a lack of private, individual space, and a threat to individual life – collective spaces are the only ones which thrive.

Passive, mass behaviour, likewise, is fatal. This is displayed mostly in the film's repeated depictions of characters watching television. President and Mrs Dale take it all for gospel, while Taffy is more cynical. The gamblers at Las Vegas are shown staring up at the television like a flock of sheep, while Richie comments on what he sees on-screen. These passive viewers conform to Claus-Dieter Rath's hypothesis of the 'socialised' viewer: 'The experience of watching television may therefore be described not so much by the words "I see," as by the words "I am among those who will have seen".'[30] An important distinguishing factor between the two types of viewer is that the independent viewer is often shown watching with the television in shot, while the passive viewers are depicted from the television point of view, as if it is watching them. In this case, the television is never in shot, functioning as the camera eye. These viewers also display the paranoia of people who expect to be watched. Robert J. Donovan and Ray Scherer consider the wonder of 'the miracle of electronics that enables mankind to be everywhere instantly ... the technology needed to send pictures and messages across national boundaries'.[31] This is very convenient, but it is also the ultimate invasion.

Repeatedly in *Mars Attacks!* television is in control. Plot developments cut to characters watching them on television, until the characters – and the audience – cannot distinguish immediately between television and 'reality', and sometimes do not wish to. When Billy Glenn Norris, volunteer soldier, is shot by a Martian on live television, his father punches buttons on the remote control muttering 'That didn't happen ...'. Similarly, a sequence where the Martians destroy or mutilate one monument after another ends with a shot of Godzilla rampaging through skyscrapers. The shot then widens to show that Godzilla is on television, and widens again to show the Martians watching, then changing channel to *The Dukes of Hazzard*. Thus technology even invades and deceives sensory evidence, reminiscent of Sontag's assertion of science fiction film's capacity for 'sensuous elaboration' as its main advantage over literature.[32]

Mars Attacks! shows not just the consumers but also the creators of television, often the same people: Nathalie Lake and Jason Stone are TV journalists/presenters, while President Dale is master of the moving political speech. But his relationship with television does not have the reciprocal naive sweetness attributed to Ronald Reagan, who 'learned a lot from television about how what he was doing affected people' and 'was especially affected by tales of tribulation affecting an individual', to the point of changing policies.[33] Reagan's conception of television seems to be as guide, philosopher and friend, while Dale divides the medium into the good, friendly camera and the TV receiver which is the harbinger of doom. The TV controllers want to present a slick, perfect show, but the Martians constantly undermine them. Claus-Dieter Rath considers live television as impure: 'in a live broadcast, footage which would have been cut out of a recording will actually get aired ... The live broadcast is an "impure" broadcast.'[34] From this viewpoint, the Martians introduce impurities into the broadcasts. However, the television which they produce is compelling, complete with its own special effects. The passive viewers are glued to the screen. One of the signs that the Martians are not 'civilised' is that they produce wonderful real disaster television. President Dale's TV appearances are meticulously orchestrated, but he cannot hope to match the impact of the Martians who, quite literally, steal the show. This alien mastery of the form implies television's invasive extraterrestrial status.

Wells's novel and Burton's film show a variety of influences, sometimes seeming, especially in the case of *Mars Attacks!*, more like a patchwork of genres than a cohesive text. Several critics have seen *The War of the Worlds* as borrowing from and extending a range of genres, in Wells's creation of a whole new genre. John Batchelor compares *The War of the Worlds* to the invasion novel,[35] a form effectively dating from *The Battle of Dorking* in 1871, in which Germany destroys a Home Counties community.[36] Wells's meticulous mapping of Surrey draws on the specificity of this work, but his choice of Mars as the external aggressor makes other invasion novels seem parochial.[37]

Herbert L. Sussman generalises: 'the scientific romances are adaptations of the imperialistic adventure story to the problem of the machine',[38] which is both ingenious and plausible. Wells himself made some scathing comments on the genre when reviewing *Heart of the World* by H. Rider Haggard:

> very little boys like to identify themselves with a successful 'bounder' of the type of the Rider Haggard hero. Whether it is good for them is another matter ... it must fill their heads with very silly ideas about the invulnerability and other privileges of the Englishman abroad.[39]

At this point Wells was writing *The War of the Worlds*.[40] It is interesting that he chooses to occupy the moral high ground, stating that reading Rider Haggard will have a bad effect on the small boys whom he scathingly identifies as the primary audience. Given the degeneration panic which to some extent informs *The War of the Worlds*, perhaps reading Rider Haggard's work had a bracing effect on Wells, encouraging him to state the case for the invaded as well as the invaders.

Wells may have been influenced by the new technology of film. In 1895 Wells and Robert Paul applied for a patent for a 'time machine', which would produce 'the sensation of voyaging upon a machine through time',[41] a theatre where an audience on moving platforms would see slides and motion pictures produced by projectors on moving tracks, allowing dramatic changes in scale and perspective.[42] The project, which was never realised, was suggested by *The Time Machine*, where time itself is like a reel of film, and the Time Machine is the camera which can run it backwards and forwards at will. Wells's descriptions of action and scenes in *The War of the Worlds* are distinctly filmic, including close-ups, cutting quickly from one aspect of the scene to another, wide shots, views panning across the landscape, and shots which suddenly focus on the approaching Martian.

Mars Attacks!, as the latest in a long line of Martian films, shows an even wider range of reference. The plot is loosely based on *The War of the Worlds* and makes the same general assumptions: human organisation disintegrates and institutions are demolished, while the Martians, though superior in warfare, are conquered by chance. The film also reproduces the novel's images, such as the pursuing Martian in a machine, and one of the Martians' surprise appearances resembles prospectively the clip of Godzilla which is inserted in *Mars Attacks!*: 'the upper-works of a Martian fighting-machine loomed in sight over the house-tops, not a hundred yards away from us'.[43]

Mars Attacks! also draws on several films – its ambience is 1950s B-movie, while the Martian descent on Washington mirrors the saucer invasion in *Earth vs. the Flying Saucers* (Sears, 1956). Vivian Sobchack notes that such films move between 'montage and *mise en scene*',[44] and Burton's film follows the same pattern of groups of close-ups of individuals interspersed with wide-angle sweeping shots of collective Martian destruction. However, *Mars Attacks!* also parodies its very recent predecessor *Independence Day* (Emmerich, 1996). The families in the film – the President's family, a black family, and the inhabitants of a trailer in the desert – explicitly parody the earlier film's politically correct selections, while the Martians' pastime of blowing up national monuments ridicules the overused *Independence Day* trailer shot of the White House exploding.

Another inspiration was the Topps trading-card series, 'Mars Attacks!', which the official website describes as 'once considered too extreme for the marketplace'.[45] Vivian Sobchack refers to film buffs' scene-spotting as 'swapping nostalgically-remembered images like baseball trading cards',[46] and apparently *Mars Attacks!* was constructed on that basis. The official film website quotes Burton joking that '[w]e developed the script painstakingly by taking the cards and throwing them on the ground and picking out the ones that we liked'.[47] This, even as a joke, makes *Mars Attacks!* a film-buff's film.

The mixed bag of influences on both *The War of the Worlds* and *Mars Attacks!*, though, has more to do than simply keep the audience amused. Wells's and Burton's borrowing from other genres to form their works can also be seen as an act of invasion; a deliberate encapsulation of their major concern in the form of their works, and another reason why, despite the difference in genre, the two works are so fundamentally similar. Wells's and Burton's creations are simultaneously sophisticated/cynical and naive. Both texts are more or less without plot – John Batchelor states authoritatively that the novel 'depends on the careful spacing of its revelations to sustain the reader's interest',[48] while the *Guardian* dismisses *Mars Attacks!* as 'this ludicrously plotted alien-invasion comedy'.[49] The perceived audience for both is somewhat unclear; Wells is seen as a suitable author for teenage boys who read science fiction, quite apart from any adult interest, while the confusion over the intended audience for *Mars Attacks!* is shown by the video's trailers: *Space Jam, Babylon 5, Father's Day* and *Batman & Robin* – kids' film or 'proper' science fiction? Yet despite the possibility of the randomness induced by throwing trading-cards on the ground, *Mars Attacks!* maintains the conventional structural models of science fiction invasion film. William Johnson posits a four-stage structure of war, anarchy, reconstruction and a new society,[50] while Susan Sontag's most pertinent scenario is a five-phase model of arrival, confirmation via destruction, conferences, further atrocities and more conferences leading to final repulse.[51] Johnson's model is mainly intended to describe 'serious' science fiction film, while Sontag's model aims at encapsulating the 'typical'; yet *Mars Attacks!* fits into both patterns.

Both *The War of the Worlds* and *Mars Attacks!* have a not-so-hidden agenda to expose the uncertainty of civilisation, and show the aggressive invasiveness of contemporary life as a threat to what civilisation we have. The teller of both tales is a part of that invasion. The narrator of *The War of the Worlds* is finally on the side of progress and the survivor, rather than humanity, while *Mars Attacks!* is narrated not by an individual but by a film camera, blurring the boundaries of film and 'real life', just as its special effects achieve virtual reality. The last impression of both worlds after the Martian defeats is of a back-to-nature scenario: earth in ruins, uncivilised, waiting to be rebuilt. Unaccommodated humanity is finally exposed, but its landscape is alien.

Notes

1. George E. Slusser and Eric S. Rabkin (eds), *Aliens: The Anthropology of Science Fiction* (Carbondale, IL: Southern Illinois University Press, 1987), p. vii.

2. Richard Hodgens, 'A Brief, Tragical History of the Science Fiction Film' in William Johnson (ed.), *Focus on the Science Fiction Film* (Englewood Cliffs, NJ: Prentice-Hall, 1972), p. 81.

3. Susan Sontag, *Against Interpretation and Other Essays* (London: Eyre and Spottiswoode, 1987), pp. 212–13.

4. H.G. Wells, *The War of the Worlds* (1898), ed. and intro. David Y. Hughes and Harry M. Geduld (Bloomington, IN: Indiana University Press, 1993), p. 151.

5. Ibid., p. 150.

6. Zoe Sofia, 'Aliens 'R' U.S.: American Science Fiction viewed from Down Under' in Slusser and Rabkin, *Aliens*, p. 113.

7. Winfried Baumgart, *Imperialism: The Ideal and the Reality of British and French Colonial Expansion, 1880–1914* (Oxford: Oxford University Press, 1982), p. 82.

8. Cited in Bernard Bergonzi, *The Early H.G. Wells* (Manchester: Manchester University Press, 1961), p. 135.

9. Baumgart, *Imperialism*, pp. 83, 87.

10. Ibid., p. 90.

11. C.C. Eldridge, *Victorian Imperialism* (London: Hodder and Stoughton, 1978), pp. 211–12.

12. Wells, *The War of the Worlds*, p. 52.

13. Patrick Moore, *Guide to Mars* (London: Frederick Muller Ltd., 1956), pp. 112–13.

14. Patrick Parrinder, 'H.G. Wells and the Fiction of Catastrophe', *Renaissance and Modern Studies*, 28 (1984), p. 57.

15. Wells, *The War of the Worlds*, p. 121.

16. Ibid., p. 67.

17. Ibid., p. 102.

18. Ibid., p. 185.

19. Bergonzi, *The Early H.G. Wells*, p. 131.

20. Ibid., p. 192.

21. Ibid., p. 174.

22. Anne B. Simpson, 'The "Tangible Antagonist": H.G. Wells and the Discourse of Otherness', *Extrapolation*, 31:2 (Summer 1990), p. 142.

23. Jonathan Romney, 'Art Forms of the Century: Terminated?', *Guardian*, 21 December 1996, p. 6.

24. In both texts nameless characters predominate: in *The War of the Worlds* the narrator, his wife, his brother, the curate and artilleryman, the five main characters, are all unnamed, while the cast list of *Mars Attacks!* has only twenty-seven named parts out of seventy-one (most of the unnamed parts are listed as job descriptions).

25. Norman and Jeanne Mackenzie, *The Life of H.G. Wells: The Time Traveller* (1973), revised edn (London: Hogarth Press, 1987), p. 32.

26. Wells, *The War of the Worlds*, p. 55.

27. Ibid., p. 55.

28. Mackenzie, *The Life of H.G. Wells*, p. 113.

29. Wells, *The War of the Worlds*, p. 192.

30. Claus-Dieter Rath, 'Live Television and its Audiences: Challenges of Media Reality' in Ellen Seiter, Hans Borchers, Gabriele Kreutzner and Eva-Maria Warth (eds), *Remote Control: Television, Audiences, and Cultural Power* (London: Routledge, 1991), p. 89.

31. Robert J. Donovan and Ray Scherer, *Unsilent Revolution: Television News and American Public Life, 1948–1991* (Cambridge: Cambridge University Press, 1992), p. 318.

32. Sontag, *Against Interpretation*, p. 212.

33. Donovan and Scherer, *Unsilent Revolution*, p. 179.

34. Rath, 'Live Television and its Audiences', p. 80.

35. John Batchelor, *H.G. Wells* (Cambridge: Cambridge University Press, 1985), p. 7.

36. I.F. Clarke (ed.), *The Tale of the Next Great War, 1871–1914* (Liverpool: Liverpool University Press, 1995), pp. 27–73.

37. Clarke lists eight other invasion novels which appeared in 1898. These include *Anglo-Saxons Onward!*, *The War of the Wenuses*, *What Will Japan Do?* and *The Yellow Danger*, most of which seem to have jingoism as their driving force – and express contemporary anxieties about Britain's capacity to defend itself. I.F. Clarke, *Voices Prophesying War 1763–1984* (London: Oxford University Press, 1966), p. 233.

38. Herbert L. Sussman, *Victorians and the Machine: The Literary Response to Technology* (Cambridge, MA: Harvard University Press, 1968), p. 183.

39. H.G. Wells in Patrick Parrinder and Robert M. Philmus (eds), *H.G. Wells's Literary Criticism* (Brighton, Sussex: Harvester Press, 1980), p. 98. This review first appeared in the *Saturday Review*, 30 May 1896.
40. Hughes and Geduld, introduction to *The War of the Worlds*, p. 1.
41. John Barnes, *The Beginnings of the Cinema in England* (New York: Barnes and Noble, 1976), p. 38.
42. John L. Fell, *Film and the Narrative Tradition* (Berkeley: University of California Press, 1986), p. 82; Brooks Landon, *The Aesthetics of Ambivalence: Rethinking Science Fiction Film in the Age of Electronic (Re)Production* (Westport, CN: Greenwood Press, 1992), pp. xiv–xv.
43. Wells, *The War of the Worlds*, p. 143.
44. Vivian Carol Sobchack, *The Limits of Infinity* (South Brunswick and New York: A.S. Barnes and Co., 1980), p. 137.
45. http://www.marsattacks.com (Warner Brothers).
46. Sobchack, *Limits of Infinity*, p. 64.
47. http://www.marsattacks.com (Warner Brothers).
48. Batchelor, *H.G. Wells*, p. 25.
49. *Guardian*, 20 December 1996, p. 21.
50. Johnson, *Focus on the Science Fiction Film*, p. 5.
51. Sontag, *Against Interpretation*, p. 210.

7

Vagabond Desire: Aliens, Alienation and Human Regeneration in Arkady and Boris Strugatsky's *Roadside Picnic* and Andrey Tarkovsky's *Stalker*

John Moore

In 1972, the major Soviet science fiction writers Arkady and Boris Strugatsky published perhaps their greatest work, a short novel entitled *Roadside Picnic*.[1] On 26 January 1973, the Soviet film-maker Andrey Tarkovsky – having just completed a successful film version of *Solaris* by the pre-eminent Polish science fiction author Stanislav Lem – wrote in his journal: 'I've just read the Strugatsky brothers' science fiction story, *Roadside Picnic*; that could make a tremendous screenplay for somebody as well.'[2] Tarkovsky, pursuing his own suggestion, became that somebody. Working with the Strugatsky brothers, who produced eleven different screenplays for the film, the great director created arguably the most sophisticated science fiction film to be made to date.[3] *Stalker*, released to great critical acclaim in 1979, 'seems to have turned out the best of all my films'.[4]

In science fiction Tarkovsky recognised an expressive form which makes possible the posing and exploration of alternatives. Such a process was necessary given the contemporaneous stifling of dissent in the Soviet bloc and the evident historical impasse of state socialism in particular and industrial civilisation in general.[5] On 7 September 1970, Tarkovsky wrote in his journal: 'The one thing that might save us is a new heresy that could topple all the ideological institutions of our wretched, barbaric world. The greatness of modern man lies in protest.'[6] In seeking this new heresy, particularly in the textual productions of his compatriots, Tarkovsky could have hardly found a more appropriate or profound work than *Roadside Picnic*. The Strugatsky brothers' novel fulfils Tarkovsky's requirements precisely because it develops a new heresy, one which postulates the project of toppling *all* ideologies and ideological institutions.

Roadside Picnic embodies a howl of protest at power, order and authority; *Stalker* transmutes the novel's violence into a more contemplative and poetic but no less trenchant and comprehensive critique of control structures. Both texts envision an uncertain, fragile but distinct possibility of total revolutionary transformation. And in both texts the science fiction trope of the (absent) alien becomes a means for bringing into focus the alienations which structure everyday life and prevent a dismantlement of power. The translation of the novel into film, however, particularly given the Strugatsky brothers' role as screenplay writers, provides a fascinating example of the process by which a shift in media can produce significantly different versions of the same scenario.

The premise upon which the narrative of *Roadside Picnic* is constructed seems at first glance to be straightforward. The novel is set in Canada in an unspecified time during the late twentieth or early twenty-first century.[7] Some thirty years before the start of the narrative, the earth has been subject to what is termed the Visitation – a brief and mysterious visitation by unknown aliens for unknown reasons. The narrative examines the effect of this event, which has in some respects changed everything, but in other respects has changed nothing whatsoever. Although of immense historical significance, the Visitation remains veiled in mystery.

The Visitation has resulted in the creation of six Visitation Zones across the world. These Zones contain various types of alien technological artefacts, which are of scientific interest, but which more importantly have possible industrial, commercial and military applications. They are thus of immense value. The Zones, however, are enormously dangerous places. In the Zones the laws of thermodynamics are randomly suspended, and various effects and conditions in a Zone can kill or maim those who enter it.

During the thirty years since the Visitation, and during the eight-year period covered by the narrative, a totalitarian hermeneutic and institutional structure has developed around the blunt facticity of the Zones' existence. The entire orientation of global society has imperceptibly shifted in response to the Visitation, although it emerges that most people remain wilfully ignorant of the momentous changes which are insidiously taking place in the world around them. As the narrative proceeds, an entire industrial, military and scientific bureaucracy, closely interlocking with organised crime syndicates and black market entrepreneurialism, gradually emerges around the six Zones.

All six sites are subject to United Nations' decisions regarding the internationalisation of the Zones. Officially, all alien technological artefacts are supposed to be retrieved by and channelled through the UN agency known as the International Institute of Extraterrestrial Cultures (IIEC). But in practice, due to the inestimable value of the artefacts to various commercial, military and criminal concerns, the Zones are regularly and illegally penetrated – despite the presence of armed military and police patrols – by nocturnal raiders working alone or in pairs and known as stalkers.

The main focus of the novel is the masculine world of the stalkers, and in particular the stalker Redrick Schuhart, who operates in the Canadian Zone of Harmont. At the beginning of the narrative, Schuhart has already served a jail sentence for stalking, and he continues to moonlight as an illegal stalker. At this stage, however, he is employed in an official capacity as a laboratory assistant and in a quasi-official capacity as a stalker by the IIEC. But when Panov, an IIEC scientist, dies after a visit to the Zone because of a mistaken judgement on Schuhart's part, Schuhart resigns his post and reverts to operating as a professional stalker.

In taking this step, Schuhart definitively places himself outside the limits of control defined by the interlocking systems of state and capital. By acting as an outlaw, he situates himself beyond legal and ethical controls, and operates as an autonomous individual who forges his own ethical code in response to changing circumstances. By refusing the category of employee, he locates himself outside the world of work and hence the disciplines of capitalist production routines. Living by his wits amid the perils of the Zone and the twilight world of organised crime, attempting to elude the attentions of the 'international police force',[8] he inhabits the narrowing margins of an increasingly totalitarian global net of 'military-industrial complexes'.[9]

The element that differentiates Schuhart from his fellow stalkers remains his class consciousness and the sociopolitical perspectives which derive from it. Unlike other stalkers, and particularly his ruthless former partner Buzzard Burbridge, Schuhart retains a fierce awareness of his working-class origins and the ways in which class relations have shaped and informed his experience. While other stalkers, and Burbridge in particular, regard the profits from stalking as a means to wealth, power, influence and class position, Schuhart has a more instrumentalist attitude to the financial income he receives from selling stolen artefacts.

In part, he believes the idealistic rhetoric that he has acquired from Panov, who maintains that the technological wonders that will result from the alien artefacts will transform human life for the better. At one point Schuhart springs to the defence of Harmont against the accusation that it is a worthless place:

> You're absolutely right. Our little town is a hole. It always has been and still is. But now it is a hole into the future. We're going to dump so much through this hole into your lousy world that everything will change in it. Life will be different. It'll be fair. Everyone will have everything that he needs. Some hole, huh? Knowledge comes through this hole. And when we have the knowledge, we'll make everyone rich, and we'll fly to the stars, and go anywhere we want. That's the kind of hole we have here.[10]

But Schuhart, although he wants to believe Panov's optimistic myth of technological progress, possesses too much knowledge about the operations of the IIEC and the criminal underworld, and about the machinations that surround the acquisition of alien artefacts, to be able fully to convince himself of the truth of the views he faithfully parrots. Further, his intimate experience of the disenablements of class – at the end of the novel he complains, 'I don't have the words, they didn't teach me the words. I don't know how to think, the bastards didn't let me learn how to think'[11] – makes him sceptical of any claims that diffusion of knowledge will include or bring benefits to him and his kind. Panov's words, although they roughly express Panov's hopes and dreams and those of his class in general, do not belong to him – no more than the artefacts that he steals from the Zone or the technological marvels that might emerge as a result. Panov's sentiments – brought to a proletarian situation from outside and above, from the idealism of a scientist of the bureaucratic class – do not match the realities of day-to-day working-class existence. And it is when Schuhart negotiates these realities that his instrumental attitude toward the money he makes from the artefacts becomes apparent. Rather than using his income to accommodate himself to the hegemonic social formation, Schuhart uses it to open up space and minimise his dependency on the formation's work routines and disciplines.

If Schuhart is of proletarian origin, his class identity is congruent not with the domesticated, integrated sectors of the working class, but with its unruly, resistant elements. During perhaps his final trip into the Zone, a smell involuntarily recalls a childhood memory and results in a kind of perverse proletarian Proustian epiphany:

> It took a while to understand that the stench was coming from himself. The odor was disgusting, but somehow familiar – that was the smell that filled the city on the days that the north wind carried the smoke from the plant. And his father smelled that way too, when he came home, hungry, gloomy, with red wild eyes. And Redrick would hurry to hide in some faraway corner and watch in fear as his father tore off his work clothes and tossed them to his mother, pulled off his huge, worn shoes and shoved them on the floor of the closet, and stalked off to the shower in his stocking feet, leaving sticky footprints.[12]

Schuhart remembers that it was only after his father had bathed and begun eating that he dared to 'climb up on his lap, and ask which shop steward and which engineer he had drowned in vitriol that day'.[13] The red-haired Schuhart, his forename shortened to 'Red', is associated with his red-eyed father through their common smell, their shared hatred of labour, and their common rebellion – whether against unions or bosses. The connection between father and son, particularly in their common refusal of work, becomes explicit when Schuhart mentally addresses his collective enemies:

> Get a job? I don't want to work with you, your work makes me puke, do you understand? This is the way I figure it: if a man works with you, he is always working for one of you, he is a slave and nothing else. And I always wanted to be myself, on my own, so that I could spit at you all, at your boredom and despair.[14]

Offered the opportunity of a new life through emigration to Europe, Schuhart violently rejects this possibility, telling the emigration agent, 'I know about your boredom. You knock yourself out all day, and watch TV all night.'[15]

Schuhart's affirmation of his self and its lived authenticity over the world of work, alienation and coercion remains reminiscent of Max Stirner. In other respects too Schuhart recalls the thought of the original anarchist individualist. Although of working-class parentage, Schuhart rejects the labouring life of his father. Stirner makes a distinction between two sectors within the proletariat. On the one hand there are labourers who remain within the ruling parameters of work, morality, lifestyle and the law. On the other hand, Stirner refers to what he terms vagabonds:

> All these lack settlement, the *solid* quality of business, a solid, seemly life, a fixed income etc.; in short, they belong, because their existence does not rest on a *secure basis*, to the dangerous 'individuals or isolated persons', to the dangerous *proletariat*; they are 'individual bawlers' who offer no 'guarantee' and have 'nothing to lose', and so nothing to risk ... All who appear to the commoner suspicious, hostile,

and dangerous might be comprised under the name 'vagabonds'.[16]

Having witnessed how work transformed his father into a figure of anguish, taciturnity and impotent rage, Schuhart chooses the life of the vagabond – that social class dismissively rejected by Marx as the lumpenproletariat – rather than the life of the wage slave. By rejecting the world of work Schuhart becomes a true stalker – not merely of alien artefacts but, in the end, of the society he inhabits. Preferring the risks of the Zone and the insecurities of the vagabond lifestyle to the stultifying routines of the planetary work-machine, Schuhart embraces the role of stalker. He has an innate hatred of the systems that constrain him and a restlessness of movement that brings perpetual dissatisfaction. In his head he contests the points made by his obese bureaucrat acquaintance, Richard Noonan:

> Noonan's a fool: Redrick, Red, you violate the balance, you destroy the order, you're unhappy, Red, under any order, any system. You're not happy under a bad one, you're not happy under a good one. It's people like you who keep us from having the Kingdom of Heaven on Earth. What do you know, fatso? Where have you seen a good system? When have you ever seen me under a good system?[17]

The sub-text of Schuhart's thought is the growing realisation that it is not a question of whether any one order or system is good or bad. The notions of order and system in themselves need to be rejected. Schuhart emerges as a profoundly anti-systemic, anti-ideological, anarchic figure, who seeks redemption in the chaos – the anarchy – of the Zone rather than the world of coercion and control. Or to put it more accurately, he becomes a figure who ultimately seeks the key to ending the world of coercion and control by entering the chaotic interior of the Zone and of his self.

The narrative of *Roadside Picnic* converges on the ultimate quest. Stalker lore tells of the existence in the Zone of a Golden Ball, which possesses the capacity to grant one's deepest wish. Buzzard Burbridge has located the Ball, but – crippled on an earlier journey into the Zone with Schuhart – he is unable to claim it for himself. There is, however, no evidence that the artefact possesses the capacity mythically accorded to it (particularly given that artefacts recovered from the Zone are notorious for the unpredictability and inexplicability of their properties). But the textual implication remains that in the Zone – the realm of irrationality, the unconscious – faith in the miraculous nature of the Golden Ball is sufficient to engender in the Ball the desired magical capacity.

Schuhart, having pared away the remnants of ideology by the end of the narrative, reaches a point at which he is able to confront with relative clarity the nature of his desire. Ostensibly, Schuhart's quest for the Golden Ball concerns the search for a cure for the anguish, suffering and alienation experienced by his daughter, Monkey. The children of stalkers are born with certain mutations. Schuhart's daughter, Maria, is affectionately known as Monkey because she is covered by golden fur, which is at one point characterised as a 'golden fleece'.[18] During the course of the narrative she also loses the capacity (or perhaps the will) to speak. This development may be related to the distinctly incestuous overtones that characterise the relationship between Schuhart and Monkey.[19] Schuhart's love, concern and desire for Monkey impel his quest in search of the Golden Ball, perhaps in search of a desired sexual union, perhaps in search of a reconciliation and healing of the wounds caused by his sexual desire, or perhaps both. Psychologically, Schuhart seeks to heal both his and Monkey's suffering, not least by overcoming the barrier between them. He has never acquired, and she loses, the capacity for expressing desires. Language, in different ways, fails them both. But the colour symbolism clearly links Monkey's golden fur with the Golden Ball, and for Schuhart the attainment of one correlates with the attainment of the 'other ' (in both senses of the word). Desire is the fulcrum, as Schuhart tells Artie: 'The Golden Ball grants your deepest, innermost wishes, the kind that if they're not granted, it's all over for you!'[20]

Such is the compelling need which drives Schuhart's desire that during the quest for the Golden Ball the altruistic stalker ruthlessly sacrifices Artie – Burbridge's beloved only son – for

Monkey's sake: 'My choice is always either/or. He finally understood the choice: either this boy, or my Monkey. There was no real choice, it was clear.'[21] Nevertheless there is a distinctly sociopolitical dimension to this decision. Artie was being groomed by his father to be a lawyer, perhaps a cabinet member, maybe even president. For Schuhart, the future can only hold either Monkey – the symbol of otherness, difference and unbounded desire – or Artie, the prospective embodiment of law and the state.

When it comes to articulating his desires to the Golden Ball, however, the inarticulate man of action and violence, who has been excluded from the world of language and intellect by his class position, can find no better way of phrasing his deepest desire than in the words of the hapless Artie as he heedlessly rushed, apparently toward the Ball, but actually towards his death. And so the narrative ends with Schuhart hoping that the Ball can read his heart and relying on his personal integrity and autonomy to guarantee the rightness of his desire:

> Look into my heart. I know that everything you need is in there. It has to be. I never sold my soul to anyone! It's mine, it's human. You take from me what it is I want ... it just can't be that I would want something bad! Damn it all, I can't think of anything, except these words of his ... 'HAPPINESS FOR EVERYBODY, FREE, AND NO ONE WILL GO AWAY UNSATISFIED.'[22]

Schuhart's desire for Monkey expands to encompass a request for universal happiness, fulfilment and the satisfaction of desire for all humanity. Earlier, he decided: 'Everything had to be changed. Not one or two lives, not one fate or two – every link in this rotten, stinking world had to be changed.'[23]

Whether this project represents Schuhart's heart's desire and whether his faith in the innate goodness of his desire is justified remain unknown; hence the outcome of his wish remains unknown.

Tarkovsky's *Stalker* revises and reworks numerous aspects of *Roadside Picnic*. The protagonist – merely known as Stalker – only enters into the Zone once during the film. No artefacts are mentioned and money remains a peripheral concern; the Golden Ball is replaced by a Room where wishes come true. The stalker is recast in the role of a guide for seekers after the truth. In the narrative, he guides two men – merely known (presumably for security reasons) as Writer and Professor after their respective professions – to the Room. But the narrative appears to be one of failure, as neither figure has the courage to enter the Room, and Stalker returns from the Zone in despair, bemoaning the faithlessness of modern human.

As Maya Turovskaya notes, however, 'the most important and decisive change' effected in the translation of fiction into film remains the 'change in the Stalker himself'.[24] In *Roadside Picnic* Schuhart is characterised by his violence, his massive physique and his working-class anger. But in Tarkovsky's film, Stalker is a slightly-built, weak, *déclassé* figure. On the threshold of the Room, the Professor reveals that he has brought a bomb with him to destroy the Zone, fearing that the Room's capacity to grant wishes could cause a catastrophe if it is activated by 'would-be emperors, Grand Inquisitors, Führers of all shades. The so-called saviours of mankind.'[25] Three times Stalker tries to disarm Professor, and each time Writer easily throws him to the ground. Stalker feebly protests: 'There's nothing else left to people on earth. This is the only ... the only place to come to when all hope is gone. You have to come here. Then why destroy hope?' When Writer then accuses Stalker of being a 'hypocritical louse' who never enters the Room himself because '[h]ere you're tsar and God ... You're drunk with power out here. What further desires can there be?', Stalker self-pityingly defends himself. A close-up shot of Stalker's tearful face accompanies his choked-up account of himself:

> Yes, I'm a louse. I've never achieved anything. I can't do anything here. I have nothing to give my wife. I can't have any friends, but don't deprive me of what's mine. They've already taken everything from me behind the barbed wire. Everything I have is here. Here, in the Zone. My happiness, my freedom, dignity: they're all here. The people I bring here are as unhappy and wretched as I am. They've nothing left to hope for. Nobody can help them. But I, a louse, can. I can weep for joy because I can help them; I ask for nothing more.

Stalker's wish doesn't come true: he cannot help the people he guides through the Zone. Because of their lack of faith he finds it impossible to give them any hope. Nonetheless, Writer's apologetic response remains significant: 'Well, you're simply one of God's fools.' This point is echoed by Stalker's wife after her husband's return from the Zone. Addressing the camera, she comments: 'You've probably already guessed that he's one of God's fools. Everyone around here used to laugh at him, he was such a wretched muddler.'

Rather than the proletarian brawler of *Roadside Picnic*, the film's protagonist is cast in the archetypal Russian role of the holy fool, the weak man whose innocence and powerlessness remain his source of strength. As Tarkovsky remarked in his journal on 29 December 1976, while making the film, '*Stalker* is from the word "to stalk" – to creep.'[26] Stalker's renunciation of force embodies his anti-authoritarianism and remains commensurate with his goal of selflessly leading others toward self-realisation.

In *Sculpting in Time: Reflections on the Cinema*, Tarkovsky comments that his films concern 'people possessed of *inner* freedom despite being surrounded by others who are inwardly dependent and unfree; whose apparent weakness is born of moral conviction and a moral standpoint and in fact is a sign of strength'. And further, that 'The Stalker seems to be weak, but essentially it is he who is invincible because of his faith and will to serve others.'[27] This point is reiterated in a central moment in the film when, on the threshold of the house which contains the Room, Stalker prays for success. While the camera focuses downwards vertically on an illuminated disc of subtly shifting quicksilver, Stalker intones an entreaty which intermixes scriptural references to Christ's emphasis on childlike gentleness with passages from the *Tao te Ching* which stress the importance of softness:

> May everything come true. May they believe ... But, above all, may they believe in themselves and become as helpless as children for softness is great and strength is worthless. When a man is born, he is soft and pliable. When he dies, he is strong and hard. When a tree grows it is soft and pliable. But when it is dry and hard, it dies. Hardness and

strength are death's companions. Flexibility and softness are the embodiment of life. That which has become hard shall not triumph.

These religious references might suggest that, in contrast to *Roadside Picnic*, the politics of *Stalker* remain conservative at best. But this is not the case. Although a very different figure from Schuhart, Stalker still remains a focus for radical vision. Imprisonment remains a key issue. In a passage quoted above, Stalker remarks: 'They've already taken everything from me behind the barbed wire.' On reaching the Zone, Professor tells Writer that Stalker has been 'imprisoned several times'. At the end of the film Stalker's wife refers to her husband as a 'marked man' and 'an eternal jailbird'. And at the beginning of the film, when she tries to stop him from entering the Zone by saying, 'You intended to do some proper work. They promised you a decent, normal job', Stalker echoes Rousseau's 'Man was born free, and everywhere he is in chains' by remarking: 'Jail. But I'm imprisoned everywhere. Let me go.'

A crucial moment of revelation concerning the imprisonment of Stalker occurs after the exhausted and despairing protagonist returns to his home at the end of the film. The camera focuses on Stalker as he lies on his side on a bare wooden floor and complains about Writer and Professor's nihilism: 'And they still call themselves the intelligentsia; writers and scientists ... They don't believe in anything. Their capacity for faith has atrophied for lack of use.' The camera then pans back to reveal a wall completely covered with shelves of books. More books are revealed as Stalker's wife helps him across the room and into bed. In an instant, the significance of the contemplative Stalker, a brooding figure who quotes poetry and scripture on his journey through the Zone, is made clear.

Stalker's imprisonment relates as much to his intellectual or artistic dissidence as to his penetrations of the Zone; or, to put it another way, the quests into the Zone serve in part as metaphors for dissident cultural activity. As Mark Le Fanu comments: 'Stalker, with his shaved head and quasi-convict gear (we learn that he has been in jail previously) is the image of one of Solzhenitsyn's "Zeks".'[28] Stalker is an inhabitant of the Gulag Archipelago and along with other contemporary artist-intellectual dissidents such as Solzhenitsyn, he realises that it is the entirety of modern society, and not merely the internment camps themselves, that has become a prison.

Stalker, then, is not the angry, violent proletarian of *Roadside Picnic*. He is not a vagabond. But he does match the type of unruly intellectuals with which Stirner complements this category:

> For there are intellectual vagabonds too, to whom the hereditary dwelling-place of their fathers seems too cramped and oppressive for them to be willing to satisfy themselves with the limited space any more: instead of keeping within the limits of a temperate style of thinking, and taking as inviolable truth what furnishes comfort and tranquility to thousands, they overlap all bounds of the traditional and run wild with their impudent criticism and untamed mania for doubt, these extravagating vagabonds. They form the class of the unstable, restless, changeable, of the *proletariat*, and, if they give voice to their unsettled nature, are called 'unruly fellows'.[29]

Stalker remains unsatisfied by the 'limited space' of the Soviet domain and seeks an alternative space in the prohibited, militarily guarded area of the Zone. He refuses to take as 'inviolable truth what furnishes comfort and tranquility to thousands' – in this instance, the doctrine of Marxism. Where he differs from Stirner's representation is that he emerges less as a figure of negation – of criticism and doubt – than as one of affirmation – of faith and belief in miracles.

Stalker certainly frames his resistance in spiritual and largely Christian terms, but these are terms of radical antinomianism rather than the moral dictates and self-renunciations of orthodox Christianity. When Writer asks whether the Zone lets the good through its complex maze of traps but kills the evil, Stalker replies: 'I'm not sure. I think it lets those through who've lost all hope; not good or bad, but the wretched. But even the wretched will perish here if they don't know how to behave.' Stalker – like the Zone, the place which he calls 'home' – does not think in moral terms, but in terms of appropriate conduct. The Zone lets Writer and Professor through to the Room, despite their errors and regardless of their failings as individuals, as (allegorical) representatives of the arts and sciences, and as members of a debased intelligentsia. Stalker and the Zone offer the possibility of redemption, but the socio-intellectual scion of Soviet society remains incapable of accepting the offer. As Stalker comments to his wife on his return: 'You saw them. Their eyes are blank. All the time they're thinking how not to sell themselves cheaply ... how to get a higher price, how to get paid for every breath they take. They were "born to be someone", the "elite", the "chosen few". They repeat: "You only live once." How can such people believe in anything at all .... Nobody believes. Not only those two.' Stalker's impoverished *déclassé* status fuels his bitterness at the nihilism of the *nomenklatura* – the privileged elite which shapes Soviet society, and yet remains imbricated in materialism and commodification. The inability of the intelligentsia even to believe in the possibility of desire coming true and thus effecting total transformation condemns them to perpetual failure and the Stalker to despair.

Tarkovsky recognises in this despair the potential for the development of Stalker from an anti-authoritarian into a profoundly authoritarian figure. In his journal entry for 28 January 1979, Tarkovsky postulated the possibility of a sequel:

> How about developing *Stalker* into a subsequent film – still with the same actors?
> Stalker starts forcibly to drag people to the Room and turns into a 'votary', a 'fascist'. 'Bullying them into happiness.'
> Can it be done that way? Bullying them into happiness ... Those who shatter the foundations – how are they engendered?[30]

Like *Roadside Picnic*, *Stalker* develops into a meditation on the nature and utopian possibilities of happiness. But unlike the euphoric though uncertain affirmation of universal happiness and fulfilled desire at the close of the novel, the film ends on a far more ambivalent note. Schuhart's radical attempt to 'shatter the foundations' may have a chance for success, but Stalker's attempt seems to have ended in failure, and the ensuing despair could open the way to the totalitarian use of force to make people happy. Tarkovsky remains profoundly aware of the dangers inherent in any totalising desire for happiness – which takes away any possibility of hope – and this recognition emerges in Writer's sour comment to Stalker in the Zone: 'I see you've decided to smash humanity with some inconceivable boon.' Further, toward the end of the film, Stalker's wife affirms her relationship with her husband – despite all its tribulations – precisely on the grounds of its emotional ambivalence: 'I was sure I'd be happy with him. I knew there'd be a lot of sorrow but I'd rather know bitter-sweet happiness than a grey, uneventful life ... And if there were no sorrow in our lives, it wouldn't be better. It would be worse. Because then there'd be no happiness either. And there'd be no hope.' So Stalker's sense of loss at the failure of his quest to initiate universal happiness seems misplaced.

But in fact, unbeknownst to the film's protagonist, events have outpaced him, and his unconscious wishes are coming true. The story of the stalker Porcupine is slowly revealed during the journey through the Zone. After his brother was maimed in the Zone, Porcupine asked the Room for his brother's recovery, but instead the stalker suddenly became very rich and hanged himself within days. Writer comes to realise the significance of this story: 'He [Porcupine] realized that it is one's most secret wish that is granted here ... Here will come true that which reflects the essence of your true nature ... it is within you, it governs you, yet you are ignorant of it ... Porcupine was given the true essence of his nature.' The division between conscious wish and unconscious desire, and the consequent lack of self-knowledge, remains responsible for the lack of nerve which prevents Writer and Professor from entering the Room. As Writer comments: 'How can I put a name to what I want? How am I to know I don't really want what I want or that I really don't want what I don't want ... My conscious mind wants vegetarianism to triumph all over the world. My subconscious longs for a juicy steak. So what do I want?' But as Stalker later comments, '[t]here's no need to speak' in the Room. Articulation of desire remains unnecessary because the Zone, symbol of the unconscious, has immediate access to any individual's subconscious wishes.

Stalker's desire for Monkey's recovery – in the film she is crippled – remains unspoken throughout the movie, although the parallel situation with Porcupine and his brother remains implicit. And any sexual desire he has for his daughter is even less tangible, limited to the opening scene when Stalker watches Monkey as she sleeps in the bed. Nevertheless the narrative converges on the apparently marginal figure of Monkey.

Tarkovsky makes significant use of colour in *Stalker*. The sequence prior to arrival in the Zone is shot in black and white to render the monochrome nature of the bleak urban wasteland of industrial civilisation. In contrast, the sequence in the Zone is shot in colour to stress the beauty of its verdant natural landscape. At one point, while the three questers rest before entering the house in the Zone, Stalker falls asleep while Writer and Professor continue their sterile cerebral conversations. The ensuing dream sequence – in which a female voice whispers a passage from the Apocalypse and laughingly rejoices at the prospect of the overthrow of power and authority – is shot in golden sepia. In close-up, the camera pans over a shallow tiled pool which is littered with the detritus of Western civilisation. At this point, both in the dream and in waking life, a black alsatian dog joins Stalker. Later, back in the bar from which the expedition into the Zone commenced, the sequence is shot in golden sepia. Stalker leaves the bar with his wife, Monkey – and the dog, which has followed him out of the Zone. Outside, the camera focuses on Monkey, whom Stalker carries home on his shoulders through the bleak industrial wasteland. But this sequence is shot in colour and for the first time it becomes apparent that Monkey wears a golden shawl – the colour linking her with the Zone – wrapped tightly around her head. Back in Stalker's apartment, the sequence of Stalker's despair and his wife's affirmation of their bittersweet life is shot in golden sepia. But the film's final sequence, focusing again on Monkey, is shot in colour, even though it is set in the apartment's interior.

Tarkovsky's use of chromatics symbolises the changes that are taking place beyond Stalker's ken. Although he does not realise it, Stalker's communion with his unconscious/the Zone *does* result in his dream coming true – a dream which combines a desire for Monkey's recovery and social transformation. It is just that, as Writer remarks, 'You dream of one thing and get something quite different.' The world *is* subtly transformed on Stalker's return from the Zone: interiors are suffused with the golden hues associated with the unconscious, and the golden-shawled Monkey is represented, like the Zone, in full colour. Symbolically, the dog – foregrounded by the camera but barely noticed by Stalker – is the vehicle by which the wonders of the Zone are transported into the outside world.

At the end of the film, as his wife helps the broken Stalker into bed, wind-borne seeds begin to waft into the room. The camera then switches to Monkey reading a book. The book establishes the vital link between father and daughter, and their shared dissidence. As more airborne seeds drift around her, we hear Monkey's voice for the first and only time as she mentally recites a poem by the nineteenth-century Russian poet Fyodor Tyuchev. The poem concerns desire, and sexual desire in particular, as the speaker admires the power of the beloved's eyes in the moment they are downcast for a passionate kiss, 'When through lowered eyelids glows/The sombre, dull flame of desire'. Spring, figured in the seeds, finally arrives in the wasteland of industrial civilisation, and with it arrives hope for the wasteland's supersession. Desire is the last word uttered in the film.

In the closing sequence, Monkey telekinetically moves three glass containers – one holding a cracked-open eggshell – across a tabletop, an action at one point symbolically counterpointed by a whine from the dog, the emblem of the Zone. At the time of the film's premiere, Tarkovsky talked of his belief in the telekinetic potential of future generations.[31] Clearly, however, the image of telekinesis need not be interpreted literally, but as a metaphor for a non-ideological mode of radical social transformation.

The film ends on a bittersweet note with a fragile hint of hope for human regeneration. At various junctures, Stalker's apartment has been rocked by the passage of nearby passing trains – symbols of the dominant techno-industrial order. Each time, Tarkovsky ironically counterpoints the deafening roar of the trains by accompanying it by snatches of music embodying the triumph of bourgeois humanism and its struc-turations of liberty and desire. At the beginning of the film, the Marseillaise ironically accompanies the sound of a passing train which rattles some glass containers on a tray. At the end of the film, having moved the glass containers telekinetically, Monkey lowers her head sideways to the table as a train booms past to the equally ironic strains of Beethoven's 'Ode to Joy'.

As in *Roadside Picnic*, the die has been cast: either industrial civilisation, or the future evolutionary liberation of humanity; either the enforced social joy which papers over total immiseration, or the liberation of the bittersweet, paradoxical humanity of the other. Monkey – whether a figure of atavism or an alien mutant – remains the slender hope for the future. The film ends with the haunting image of her face. An undecidable mixture of hope and anguish, a figure of desire uncertain of fulfilment, she gazes at the camera and straight into the eyes of the viewer.

Notes

1. Arkady and Boris Strugatsky, *Roadside Picnic*, 1972 trans. Antonina W. Bouis (Harmondsworth: Penguin, 1977). M.H. Zool, in *Bloomsbury Good Reading Guide to Science Fiction* (London: Bloomsbury, 1989), p. 21, calls *Roadside Picnic* the 'most profound' novel by the Strugatskys. George Zembrowski, in *Beneath the Red Star: Studies on International Science Fiction* (San Bernardino: Borgo Press, 1996), p. 80, refers to the novel as a 'classic'.
2. Andrey Tarkovsky, *Time Within Time: The Diaries 1970–1986*, trans. Kitty Hunter-Blair (Calcutta: Seagull, 1991), p. 66.
3. Darko Suvin, 'Arkady and Boris Strugatski' in John Clute and Peter Nicholls (eds), *The Encyclopedia of Science Fiction* (London: Orbit, 1993), p. 1174.
4. Journal entry 15 April 1979, Tarkovsky, *Time*, p. 181.
5. Intensified persecution of political, intellectual and artistic dissidence was a feature of Soviet domestic policy during the late 1960s and early 1970s. Writers Andrei Sinyavsky and Yuli Daniel were sentenced in 1966 to seven and five years hard labour respectively, for writing texts deemed subversive. These convictions resulted in the rise of the dissident movement, which included prominent

writers such as Solzhenitsyn and Yevtushenko. The early 1970s witnessed a smothering of dissent in the arts due to exile, imprisonment and defection.

6. Tarkovsky, *Time*, p. 16.
7. The only specified temporal indicator relates to the award of a Nobel Prize to Dr Pilman in '19..' Arkady and Boris Strugatsky, *Roadside Picnic*, p. 11.
8. Ibid., p. 75.
9. Ibid., p. 112.
10. Ibid., p. 45.
11. Ibid., p. 160.
12. Ibid., pp. 153–4.
13. Ibid., p. 154.
14. Ibid., p. 159.
15. Ibid., p. 45.
16. Max Stirner, *The Ego and Its Own* (1845), trans. Stephen Byington (London: Rebel Press, 1993), pp. 112–13.
17. Strugatsky, *Roadside Picnic*, p. 150.
18. Ibid., p. 74.
19. The reader's first glimpse of Monkey occurs when Schuhart returns from an illegal nocturnal raid on the Zone and looks in on his daughter's bedroom: 'Monkey was sleeping peacefully, her crumpled blanket hanging on the floor. Her nightie had ridden up. She was warm and soft, a little animal breathing heavily. Redrick could not resist the temptation to stroke her back covered with warm golden fur, and was amazed for the thousandth time by the fur's silkiness and length. He wanted to pick up Monkey badly, but he was afraid it would wake her up – besides he was dirty as hell and permeated with death and the Zone' (Ibid., p. 126). This image of sexualised temptation, coded as dirty, damning and furtive, contrasts forcefully with Schuhart's impotence with his wife, Guta.
20. Ibid., p. 139.
21. Ibid., p. 144.
22. Ibid., p. 160.
23. Ibid., p. 155.
24. Maya Turovskaya, *Tarkovsky: Poetry as Cinema*, trans. Natasha Ward (London: Faber and Faber, 1989), p. 108.

25. Andrey Tarkovsky, *Stalker* (Connoisseur Video; originally released Moscow, 1979). All subsequent quotations from this film derive from the English subtitles of this release.
26. Tarkovsky, *Time*, p. 136.
27. Andrey Tarkovsky, *Sculpting in Time: Reflections on the Cinema*, trans. Kitty Hunter-Blair (London: Faber and Faber, 1989), p. 181.
28. Mark Le Fanu, *The Cinema of Andrei Tarkovsky* (London: BFI, 1987), p. 101.
29. Stirner, *Ego*, p. 113.
30. Tarkovsky, *Time*, p. 169.
31. 'Art is Created by People: Conversation with Andrey Tarkovsky after the Tallinn Première of *Stalker*', *Kino*, 11 (1979), pp. 20–2.

8

Adaptation, Teleportation and Mutation from Langelaan's to Cronenberg's *The Fly*

Karin Littau

> *Once it was human ... even as you and I ... this monster created by atoms gone wild.*
>
> Promotional caption for Neumann's *The Fly*

When Hélène Delambre describes a 'white hairy head' with 'two pointed ears', a 'pink and moist' nose with a 'black quivering trunk ... from which saliva kept dripping', she is referring, of course, to 'the monster, the thing that had been my husband'.[1] The fly-cat-man, that had been the scientist André Delambre, who is eventually killed by his wife with a steam-hammer, is a different creature in George Langelaan's short story (1957) from the species it becomes in David Cronenberg's famous remake of *The Fly* (1986). This chapter is concerned not only with the metamorphoses that the main protagonist undergoes once he has teleported himself through the 'disintegration-reintegration' machine, but also his further mutations in the different versions of the tale: that is, his teleportations as transformations of the transformation process itself. What I want to suggest is that the transmitter machine in all the fly films[2] – be it Kurt Neumann's rendition of Langelaan's story (1958), Edward Bernds's sequel, *Return of the Fly* (1959) or Cronenberg's update – might be read as a metaphor for adaptation. If the transmitter machine, as the apparatus for transporting matter from A to B, produces a monster in the process, does it follow therefore that adaptation which also transports matter from A to B equally produces a monster? What kind of baggy monster are we dealing with, then, when it comes not just to one adaptation, but a whole series of remakes?

What is apparent in all the respective tales is that the narrative gambit of renarration is foregrounded. As a nested narrative, we access Langelaan's story of André's doomed experiment from the perspective of his brother, François, whose account is based on Hélène's letter of confession, which itself is interwoven with the notes and messages written to her by her distressed fly-cat-husband because he is now no longer able to speak. Similarly, Neumann's adaptation uses the technique of flashback, thus restricting our narrative access to the events through Hélène's account, a representation of events that is in effect a subjective truth. Cronenberg, on the other hand, restructures his narrative in a linear fashion; this is also Bernds's technique, as he refers back to and retells Neumann's tale through citation. However, unlike Bernds, Cronenberg disrupts the narrative's supposed realism by accentuating both the constructedness of the narrative, and that of his main protagonist, insofar as Seth Brundle sets himself up as a narrator. While the narrative is deliberately disorientating because it moves seamlessly between 'real events' and 'dream sequences' thereby blurring the distinction, the film also continuously disrupts the cinematic illusion by drawing attention to film-making; in addition, we never forget that Brundle's account of himself and his work is narrated for the attention of Ronnie (Veronica) Quaife, a journalist for *Particle Magazine*, whose brief it is to retell his story in the form of a book.

If the narrative techniques deployed in the fly tales frustrate or undermine our immediate and unmediated access to the contents of the story, this is further amplified in the narrative content itself, where renarration is thematised not only because the characters themselves have to rely on second-hand accounts to reconstruct 'what really happened', but also because one of the core problems played out in the story itself is whether the scientist's findings are conclusive enough to be told to the world, and after his accident, whether his fateful story should be retold at all. Here, the different versions of *The Fly*, more or less, follow their own plot lines. Once the characters have the whole story, they either systematically destroy the evidence which might verify what happened in the lab (as is the case in Langelaan and Neumann), or that evidence is stolen, illicitly copied or re-edited in false hands (Bernds and Cronenberg). The characters either try to suppress the story in their effort to contain the message or they leak the story in an effort to spread the message for financial gain or professional kudos. In each case, what is at stake is the destruction of the original versus the proliferation of copies, with Langelaan and Neumann, as the 'original' producers of the story/film, appropriately thematising the former, and Bernds and Cronenberg, as the remakers, appropriately thematising the latter.

In the original story by Langelaan, Hélène's testimony of the events as they unfold is addressed to the police commissioner Charas, and thus serves as proof of her innocence. When Charas, however, burns the confession, he not only destroys the only written evidence of André's fate and his wife's sanity but, as with André's destruction of his scientific notes and his own body, he also eradicates any kind of authentic proof of the events. Equally, when Charas destroys the man-headed fly in Neumann's version of the ending (in Langelaan it is François who does the deed), the only remaining proof is crushed out of existence. What is thematised in both these versions is the destruction of the original, be it in terms of a body of texts (the letter of confession and the scientific notes) or the bodies of the 'thing' (the fly-headed André is flattened in the hydraulic press; the André-headed fly, caught in a spider's web, is squashed with a stone). In the absence of any texts, or a body, or any story which might explain the mystery, rumours spread. This, however, is not the subject of Langelaan's or Neumann's films, but of the opening sequence of Bernds's *Return of the Fly*.

This sequel, as if generated by the demand for stories, including perhaps further fly tales, begins with a scene where a journalist demands to know, now that Hélène is dead, what happened to André Delambre all those years ago. Their son Philippe also demands an explanation but, despite being told the truth by his uncle François, reiterates the line he said as a child in Neumann's version: 'I want to become an explorer like my father.' Picking up the story line where Neumann left off, Philippe shows himself intent on following in the footsteps of his father. He continues the research with the help of an employee he has poached from his uncle's firm. His new collaborator Al, alias Ronnie, turns out to be an impostor engaged in industrial espionage, who not only copies the scientific notes to sell them to the highest bidder, but also, after a struggle over the stolen manuscripts, throws Philippe in the disintegrator-reintegrator, adding a house-fly for good measure. The story repeats: Philippe has quite literally modelled himself on his father, albeit with a difference. When his fly head is eventually swapped back with the fly's human head, the status quo is preserved, not least because Philippe-cum-fly has meanwhile also managed to kill the impostor, thereby removing the interference from a non-family member. Here then, neither machinery nor scientific notes are destroyed, but the offending copyist is disposed of, so it would seem that the original is preserved. By the end of Neumann's film, however, we know that the original has been destroyed; what survives is therefore a copy (in the sense that the original has not so much been found, but reconstructed, much as Philippe finally manages to reverse the process, and undo his father-fly curse), which must defend its legitimacy by meting out justice to the illegitimate, the fly's bastard offspring.

Illicit copying is also a theme in Cronenberg's film. Not only does Ronnie Quaife secretly record (just as her namesake in Bernds's tale had done) her conversations with Brundle, who in trying to impress her lets slip rather too much of his 'change the world as we know it' invention, but she is quite willing to go to press and tell the world of this work, despite his protestations. When she shares her discoveries with her editor and ex-boyfriend, Stathis Borans, he simply discards Brundle as a con-man. The real con-man, however, turns out to be Stathis, for when he realises that Ronnie was right as to the authenticity of Brundle's invention, he snitches her story and publishes it himself; after all, he reasons when Ronnie later confronts him: 'Your discovery is my discovery.' Stathis's article for *Particle Magazine*, having been pieced together from Ronnie's recordings and the background information he himself was able to gather about Seth, is therefore written twice removed, for unlike Ronnie's first-hand account, his is second hand. Again, the copyist – here in the form of the plagiarist re-editing and leaking another's story – does not go unpunished (Brundle-Fly does not kill him, but his acidic vomit dissolves some of his body parts).

Whether Delambre's or Brundle's tales are therefore contained or silenced (the prevention of the message), or whether they are disseminated or broadcast (the proliferation of the message), what seems to be at issue here is how information can be processed: how it might on the one hand be curtailed or distorted at the source, or on the other hand be passed on, with or without interference, from one source to the next. In any given version of *The Fly* we are therefore confronted with the difficulties inherent in information flow, be this about the *source of information* (how the narrative is mediated), or the *source material* destined for later reintegration (how matter – the body itself – is mediated). This is played out in the story both at the level of narrative structure (how the reader/spectator receives the narrative information) and at the level of narrative content (how the characters learn about events, how information gets stolen, interfered with or distorted; or for that matter, how information about matter is mediated in the transmitter machine). To put this in another way, we might say that on the one hand the story raises within its own narrative structure questions to do with the mediation of narrative content and, by extension, raises issues to do with the mediation of meaning. On the other hand, the story is about the mediation of matter and therefore seizes on the medium for mediation, that is, the technical apparatus which mediates the message. What comes together in the structure and the content is the thematisation of the problematics of transmission: how to mediate the meaning of a text, and how to mediate a given text from one medium to another. What I shall pursue in the remainder of this chapter is how the story of *The Fly* itself suggests what is at stake in mediating a message from one medium to another, and how the various fly stories communicate these very concerns. Having looked at what various renarrated versions of *The Fly* tell us about story-making (or in Stathis's case, story-breaking), I shall now pose the question from a slightly different perspective: what does *The Fly* in its many transpositions tell us about the problematics of transferring a story from book to film to film?

All the fly stories are about a transmitter machine (be this called the 'disintegrator-reintegrator' or a 'teleporter'), a means of getting instantaneously from A to B by disintegrating a given source and reintegrating it at a given destination. Similarly, all the fly films are aware of their previous sources – the material, which in the process of adaptation they disintegrated, teleported and finally reintegrated into their particular version of the story. What emerges, therefore, not only within the tale, but also its retellings by its adapters, is a meta-narrative about adaptation. As such, the device of the teleportation machine featured in the narratives of *The Fly* might be taken as a trope for adaptation, or an adaptation machine, with each remake telling a different story of what gets lost, added or remains intact of the essence of the subject or object in its mediation from one medium (or 'pod') to another. As Brundle sums up the issue in Cronenberg's film: 'The computer is giving us its interpretation of a steak, it's translating it for us, rethinking it, rather than reproducing it and something is getting lost in the translation.' Since we know that André, Philippe and Seth all lose and gain something in the transmission, we might therefore also ask what gets lost and added in the tale's textual transmission. Equally, the transformation (deformation) of the scientist's body provides a kind of 'corporeal' index of the transformations throughout this body of texts.

The trope of loss and gain has haunted not only discourses about adaptation, or translation, but 'all those activities which resemble each other in that they do not resemble that from which they derive'.[3] What is at play here is a privileging of the source (the original, the model) over the target product (the version, the copy), a hierarchy between what is deemed primary, unique and pure, and what is deemed secondary, second-rate and impure. Alain Resnais gives voice to precisely this attitude when he states that 'adaptation is a little like reheating a meal',[4] a point which in the context of *The Fly* might well make us wonder whether Seth Brundle's steak in Cronenberg's adapted version tastes twice as flavourless after its teleportation as the food that André Delambre planned to transmit through his disintegration-reintegration machine in Langelaan's original version. The dictum that 'something gets lost in translation' – for Seth Brundle it is 'the poetry of steak', for Robert Frost, of course, it was simply 'poetry'[5] – illustrates the plight shared by any adaptation. 'Something important is missing' (Brundle), which is why they stand accused of having lost something essential, that which Roman Jakobson, in a different context, has also referred to as 'poeticity': the formal property which shapes a given material (form transforming content), and which 'is like oil in cooking; you cannot have it on its own but when it is used with other food it ... changes the taste of the food to the extent that some dishes no longer appear to have any connection with their oil-less counterparts'.[6] The fly texts thematise this problematic; however, they also provide, as we shall see, other tropic resources for theorising the stakes of remaking (or reheating steaks).

In Langelaan's story, as in Neumann's film, André's invention of the matter transmitter has a definite social purpose. As 'the end of all means of transport, not only of goods, including food, but also human beings',[7] the benign scientist working for humanity's welfare, working towards a world where there is no more starvation, plays with the dangers of *atoms gone wild* in a 1950s world of rapid nuclear scientific exploration. Thus, unlike Seth's telepod with which he seeks a means to overcome his own motion sickness, André's device is for the good of the species. As we know, however, things go monstrously wrong. The first inkling we have of this is when the family pet 'disintegrates perfectly, but he never reappears in the receiving set'. The 'dispersed atoms' of Dandelo, the cat, now run wild, 'God knows where, in the universe'.[8] Things get worse; for when André realises that his integration with the house-fly is irreversible (not only is the creature's head taking over his mind, but the other creature with his own head cannot be found) he finally knows that

I must destroy myself in such a way that none can possibly know what has happened to me. I have of course thought of simply disintegrating myself in my transmitter, but I might find myself reintegrated. Some day, somewhere, some scientist is sure to make the same discovery.

This day comes sooner than he might have anticipated. Urged by his wife to put himself through the transmitter once more, so that he might find himself reintegrated, the fly-man gets additionally mixed up with stray body parts of the cat. What slowly dawns on the fly-cat-man is that Dandelo, even if the original fly with his own head could be found, will still haunt the machinery, will still interfere in the matter transmitter.

Thus, it never was a question of a simple reintegration, a return of the right head on the right body, since the problem lies not in locating the fly, now buzzing in the family garden. The fault now lies in the apparatus itself, a machine ghosted by cat-atoms. In other words, the scientist – the author of the adaptation – loses control of the integrity of the material in adapting it: the process begins to run away, and the adapter's task is to rein it in. That this is impossible provides the reason, we might argue, why he destroys the apparatus. As soon as the cat has been disintegrated but has failed to be reintegrated, the machine displays a possibility that was always a threat: the reintegration might not and does not work properly. Integrity has been lost even at the level of hardware, of medium, long before the integrity of the message comes into question. To put this differently, adaptation was already a flawed venture even before anything is adapted, the medium is always a distortion – or perhaps a transformation – of the message. It is hardly a surprise then, in the final instance, that this should be the message we might receive, or decode from Langelaan's original tale.

If the medium alters the message in Langelaan's story, in Neumann's film it does not. This is because, unlike in Langelaan's story, where the interference in the machine can no longer be isolated, where the cat is in the machine ('God knows where'), in Neumann's version the transmission process is, at least after several experiments, a thorough success, and even after the mishap (very much an accident), it seems that there is still the option of isolating the interference because the fly is outside the machine. All that needs to be done is to catch the fly: 'Now my only hope is to find the fly. I've got to go through the machine once more and pray that our atoms untangle. If you [Hélène] can't find it, I have to destroy myself.' In Neumann's fim then, it is not that the machinery is flawed, but rather that control over input is lacking. The flaw here belongs to the subject, the scientist, who in a moment of carelessness, as François points out, fails to notice the fly that hitches a ride. Thus, whereas the machinery must be destroyed in Langelaan's story because the process is flawed (pathetic object), in Neumann's film the machinery must be destroyed because of the subject's lack of control to guarantee untainted, pure input (tragic subject), and because it might also fall into the wrong pair of hands. In this sense, Neumann's adaptation of *The Fly* suggests that perfect adaptation, at least in theory, is possible, given sufficient care and in the right hands, whereas Langelaan's original tale indicates that it is impossible.

Since each of the previous tales has its own 'destruction-of-evidence' story, it is as if their endings make possible further versions. Thus, in Bernds's *Return of the Fly*, we are dealing with a copy without an original, given that in Neumann's previous version, the man who became the fly went on to 'destroy everything, all evidence, even myself'. What we have in Bernds's rendition of the tale then, are the characters of Philippe and his collaborator Al (alias Ronnie), two scientists working on the transmission machine, two authors of adaptation, one authentic (following his father's footsteps), the other an impostor (disturbing the blood line). That Philippe gets amalgamated with the fly is not his fault; it is not based on human error, but is Al's deliberate deed. It would therefore be true to say that if it had not been for Al, the copyist and the trickster, there would have been no return of the fly story at all. In any case, the process is reversible. At the end we have the reintegrated Philippe, and a machine which works fine so long as it is in the right hands (and Al's were clearly the wrong ones). In this sense, *The Fly*'s come-back differentiates itself from an adaptation, for rather than merely playing on the idea that an adaptation might be parasitic on its original, just as the fly as parasite took its host for a ride, Bernds's film introduces the parasite up front: Al, the impostor, is necessary for making a sequel.

Cronenberg absorbs all the remade versions of *The Fly* in his update. Not unlike the character of Brundle-Fly himself, who absorbs and fuses with the fly at a genetic level and is therefore transformed into a new species, Cronenberg's remake in absorbing and fusing together other fly texts, does not so much faithfully reproduce recognisable aspects of each of the stories, but incorporates 'bits and pieces' from the previous versions to evolve them 'into something else'. Less an inventor than a gene-splicer, less a father than a midwife (he appears as the gynaecologist in the film),[10] less an auteur than an assembler-adapter (after all Cronenberg has adapted several literary texts), Cronenberg delivers an adaptation that is consistently aware of its own status as adaptation, a hybrid text – a *Flybrid* – 'in which a variety of writings, none of them original, blend and clash'.[11] This is why the author of the adaptation, be this Cronenberg or Brundle, is less the romantic genius than the postmodern assembler: as Cronenberg's movie has its characters say:

> Quaife: How could you do this alone?
> Brundle: Well, I don't work alone. There's a lot of stuff in there I don't even understand. I am really a system's management man. I farm bits and pieces out to the guys who are much more brilliant than I am; I say, build me a laser disc, design me a molecular analyser of that, they do, and I just stick them together, but no one knows what the project really is.

This is also why Brundle is not concerned that his work, which was sponsored by a conglomerate ('they know they'll end up owning it whatever it is'), will ultimately not be his property.

It is not Brundle's control over his invention, or his lack of control over input which matter in this version of the tale, rather, things have a way of evolving. After his fusion with the fly there is no possibility of restoring the specific integrity of the human individual or that of the insect (even if, as the computer suggests, he, Ronnie and their unborn child were to fuse, there would still be traces of fly genes in their one new body). This is a possibility that is pursued in previous versions of the tale. What the teleportation affirms is that there is no original Brundle ('I was not pure, the teleporter insisted on me being pure. I was not pure'), who may be separated neatly from the fly. It is no longer two creatures, posing as a kind of

'Cartesian opposition between mind and body',[12] but an organism which in Deleuzian-Guattarian terms is 'becoming-animal'.[13] If in Neumann's and in Bernds's films we witness a human regressing down the evolutionary ladder towards the beast (just as in these films all the scientists have to go down the stairs to their labs, be they linear as in Neumann, or spiral as in Bernds), in Cronenberg's film, the human is transforming into 'something that never existed before', going up the evolutionary ladder (like the stairs that lead to his loft),[14] displaying new strengths, new energies and even a new politics. But it is not only the human-animal hybrid that is transforming, the very apparatus for transformation itself is transformed. When the computer, as Brundle-Fly explains, 'got confused' and 'decided to splice us together' (no longer an automaton, but already an artificial intelligence?) it is hardly surprising that this machine also begins to transform itself: 'my teleporter turned into a gene-splicer'. Now that it is set up as a gene-splicer, with three rather than merely two telepods, its computer brain gets 'confused' one more time, and decides to fuse machine parts with the flesh of Brundle-Fly, thus evolving, albeit short-lived, into a cybernetic organism: 'the ultimate family' we might say (not in social but evolutionary terms) of animal, human and machine.[15]

It seems that the work of art in the age of information (whether print, digital, televisual or genetic) has fused machine and flesh, apparatus and story, medium and message. And it is by seizing the potential of this new confluence of the modes of information that Cronenberg demonstrates new possible resonances of adaptation, the evolutionary and the textual. What then does teleportation signify in Cronenberg's *The Fly*? On the one hand, the teleportation transports Brundle into a current sci-fi context (concerned less with monsters, or aliens, than with cybernetic organisms), in effect updating Langelaan's story within the genre, thus foregrounding the hardware as part of the narrative content. On the other hand, the very hardware of teleportation is adapted, remade and updated (the matter transmitter is transformed into a modern gene-splicer). Cronenberg also, however, builds the new technology into the very fabric of his picture. While all the

Delambre characters make reference to the new technologies of the media of the day (differentiating the materiality of the invention from 'electronic representation', it is said that '[w]hereas only sound and pictures had been, so far, transmitted through space by radio and television, André claimed to have discovered a way of transmitting matter'),[16] Cronenberg not only makes a hideous display of state-of-the-art special effects technology (his 'monster' is more monstrous than the actor wearing the fly helmet in Bernds's film), but also shows us through constant intercuttings to video-recorders, TV and computer screens, how adaptation itself adapts via the introduction of new technologies. Teleportation here is not simply a metaphor for adaptation which might highlight, as was the case in the previous film versions, that remakes neither transport an original faithfully, not ever leave intact that from which they derive. It becomes one of the strategies available to renarration, given the confluence of cinematic and information technology, whether it is a question of transforming bodies of texts, or quite simply, transforming bodies.

Finally, let me reflect on some of the wider issues that the teleportation device raises, not merely as regards the relationship between original text and its cinematic versions, but also as regards the different media of literature and film, the printed and the electronic. If the transmitter machine produces something 'unnatural', a monster, might we therefore assume that each and every adaptation, as the product of an 'alliance' between literature and film – which Virginia Woolf has said certainly is 'unnatural',[17] – equally produces a monster? Is Cronenberg's remake a monstrous transformation of Langelaan's story? Or is the adaptation of a literary text into the cinematic medium, appealing no longer to the finer sensibility of the imagination but to raw sensation (as genre fiction also does), a monstrous assault on its consumer? Woolf invokes a hierarchy between literature and film (which by extension also invokes one between original and adaptation, high and popular culture) which privileges the intellect. However, Mary Shelley appeals to the sensations, arguing that if *Frankenstein* (1818) did not 'speak to the mysterious fears of our nature, and awaken thrilling horror – one to make the reader dread to look around, to curdle the blood and quicken the beatings of the heart ... my ghost story would be unworthy of its name'.[18] Shelley spoke before the invention of the cinema, before her own monster's reincarnation on celluloid. But would it not be true to say that the cinema, with all the trickery and special effects at its disposal, can show us (*montrer*) what the literary text cannot? It can give form to a *monster*, not by engaging our imagination, but by affecting our physical response. As such, the horror story, and with it the hierarchy between the literary and the filmic text, is converted through film into a sequential process: from text to fright. Cronenberg knows how horror makes the blood curdle, and how cinema can give thrills that creep through the 'flesh' and excite the 'nerves'.[19] In this sense, it was never merely a question of transmitting a message from one medium (literature) to another (film), but of the transmission of matter – the bodily response. This then is the other lesson we learn from the mutations of *The Fly*: how the apparatus of the cinema in making the monster more monstrous, teleports us not simply into another imaginative space, but transmits to us something of the poetry of the flesh. In the final instance then, does this fusing of body and machine, suggestive of virtual reality, therefore already foreshadow another technology, and another, viscerally interactive, fly?

Notes

1. George Langelaan, 'The Fly', *Playboy*, June 1957, reprinted in *The Second Pan Book of Horror Stories*, ed. Herbert van Thal (London: Pan, 1960), pp. 52, 53.
2. There are two other fly films, *Curse of the Fly* (Don Sharp, 1965) and *The Fly II* (Chris Walas, 1989), which are loosely based on characters from Langelaan's story or Cronenberg's film respectively; space prevents me from looking at these versions in the present chapter.
3. Paul de Man, *Resistance to Theory* (Minneapolis: University of Minnesota Press, 1986), p. 8.
4. Quoted in Morris Beja, *Film and Literature* (New York: Longman, 1979), p. 85.

5. Robert Frost, 'Conversations on the Craft of Poetry' in Elaine Barry (ed.), *Robert Frost on Writing* (New Brunswick: Rutgers University Press 1973), p. 17.

6. This summary of Jakobson's culinary account of the relation between form and contents is given by Ann Jefferson in *Modern Literary Theory*, ed. Ann Jefferson and David Robey (London: Batsford, 1982), p. 28.

7. Langelaan, 'The Fly', p. 35.

8. Ibid., p. 38.

9. Ibid., p. 50.

10. For an argument which takes Cronenberg's cameo appearance as a comment on 'men's anxieties about creativity, and especially about controlling, keeping, and getting credit for their productions', see Helen W. Robbins' essay 'More Human than Human Alone. Womb Envy in David Cronenberg's *The Fly* and *Dead Ringers*' in Steven Cohen and Ina Rae Hark (eds), *Screening the Male: Exploring Masculinities in Hollywood Cinema*. (London: Routledge, 1993), p. 136. While Robbins sees 'his teleportation project as an attempt to give birth to himself', as a 'womb-appropriative activity' (p. 137), I see the telepod not so much as a reproductive technology that exposes anxieties about paternity and originality, but as a machine which produces, as it transports from A to B, a de-centreing and displacement between original and copy. Adaptation is not about reproduction, in the sense that it returns the self-same, but about the production of difference.

11. Roland Barthes, 'The Death of the Author' (1968), in *Image Music Text*, trans. Stephen Heath (London: Fontana, 1977), p. 146. See also Scott Bukatman's *Terminal Identity* (Durham, NC: Duke University Press, 1993), p. 268, where he makes reference to how 'the languages of Burroughs and Cronenberg commingle' in *The Fly*.

12. This point is also made by Douglas Kellner in 'David Cronenberg: Panic Horror and the Postmodern Body', *Canadian Journal of Political and Social Theory*, 13: 3 (1989), p. 89.

13. This is how Hassan Melehy describes Brundle-Fly in his 'Images Without: Deleuzian Becoming, Science Fiction Cinema in the Eighties', *Postmodern Culture*, 5: 2 (1995),

drawing on Gilles Deleuze and Félix Guattari, *A Thousand Plateaus* transl. Brian Massumi (Minneapolis: University of Minnesota Press, 1987), pp. 232–309.

14. According to Gaston Bachelard in *The Poetics of Space*, trans. Maris Jolas (Boston, MA: Beacon Press, 1969), the attic is the space of dreams, while correspondingly, the cellar is the lair of nightmares. The two spaces are indicative of the scientists' attitudes to their fly-ness. It is only Brundle who discusses its possibilities, while the Delambres bemoan its curse; it is also Brundle, echoing Kafka, who refers to dreams when he says: 'I am an insect who dreamt he was a man and loved it, but now the dream is over and the insect is awake', a comment which further puts into question what is 'real' and what is dream-sequence in the film.

15. If in both Neumann's and Bernds's fly tales women have nothing to do with the machine, in Cronenberg's both refuse to use it.

16. Langelaan, 'The Fly', p. 35.

17. Virginia Woolf, 'The Cinema' (1926), *Collected Essays*, Vol. 2 (London: The Hogarth Press, 1966), quoted by Nicola Shaughnessy in 'Is s/he or isn't s/he?: Screening *Orlando*' in Deborah Cartmell, I.Q. Hunter, Heidi Kaye and Imelda Whelehan (eds), *Pulping Fictions: Consuming Culture across the Literature/Media Divide* (London: Pluto, 1996), p. 43.

18. Mary Shelley, *Frankenstein* (3rd edn 1831), ed. Maurice Hindle (Harmondsworth: Penguin, 1992), pp. 7–8.

19. Walter Serner, 'Kino und Schaulust' (1913) in Anton Kaes (ed.), *Kino-Debatte* (Tübingen: Max Niemeyer, 1978), p. 53.

9

The *Alien* Series and Generic Hybridity

Martin Flanagan

In an international cinematic marketplace dominated by the blockbuster, the sequel has emerged as a crucial commercial strategy. The skill of keeping a franchise alive and successful over two, three or more releases has attained holy grail status among Hollywood producers. This procedure is underpinned by solid commercial logic: sequels virtually guarantee a sizeable proportion (usually at least seventy-five per cent) of the box office takings of a successful first film. Ridley Scott's *Alien* (1979) was a highly successful, not to say hugely influential film, and a sequel was inevitable. It took seven years to materialise, but James Cameron's barnstorming, militaristic *Aliens* (1986) raised the stakes of what was now a franchise in 1986. This highly profitable sequel was followed in 1992 by *Alien3*, an altogether darker affair helmed by first-time director David Fincher, which underachieved at the box office. The combination of limp commercial performance and a story line that killed off main character Ripley (Sigourney Weaver) made the prospect of another episode unlikely. However, five years later, with the formerly reluctant Weaver back on board for a rumoured $eleven million, commercial necessity triumphed and *Alien: Resurrection,* directed by Jean-Pierre Jeunet, was released to breathe new life into the saga.

The focus of this chapter will be the function of genre in a long-running Hollywood franchise. Mikhail Bakhtin conceives genre as a narrative mode which is engaged in a 'truly historical struggle' taking place over centuries of literary development, and shaped by intertextual relations and interaction with human experience in the process of reception.[1] Bakhtin talks about genres as if they were living entities, and his approach

156

seems ideally suited to the analysis of a popular Hollywood franchise such as the *Alien* cycle. In the eighteen years between *Alien* and *Alien: Resurrection*, the series acquired a life of its own, shaped by changing industrial pressures and audience patterns. The generic profiles of the first two films can be construed as reactions to shifting commercial climates. Whereas *Alien* capitalised on the horror boom of the late 1970s and early 1980s, the market had changed by 1986. The horror genre, represented by such lamentable efforts as *Friday the 13th Part VI: Jason Lives* (Tom McLoughlin, 1986), was waning, but action vehicles such as *Rambo: First Blood Part II* (George P. Cosmatos, 1985) and *Commando* (Mark L. Lester, 1985) were cleaning up at the box-office. *Aliens* reflected this trend in the presence of action virtuoso James Cameron as writer-director.

Industrial factors such as these have crucial repercussions at the level of film narrative. The process by which the text is shaped by its interaction with social and historical forces is of primary importance to the Bakhtinian project, as the concept of dialogism illustrates. Dialogism describes how all language usage depends on the anticipated response of the other. The utterance is implicitly 'dialogic', in that it is tailored around and shaped by this response, ultimately creating a chain of meaning whereby each word carries the inflections of all its previous usages in any number of social situations. If we consider the film text as a form of textual 'utterance', we can see that the same rules apply. The understanding of the cinematic spectator denotes the response necessary for the text to communicate its narrative message. The formulation of reception suggested by dialogic theory raises the spectator to a position of active participation in the textual process, and we can see how this kind of relationship underwrites marketing strategies such as the test screening. The screening is a microcosmic version of the way that commercial cinema functions in relation to its audience; films that fail to convey their message in a way that is narratively comprehensible and pleasing to a general audience invariably underperform at the box office. This is where genres come in, providing a coherent framework and recognisable signifying system for varied narrative material. But the parameters of these generic frameworks are subject to constant change: what constituted a horror film thirty years ago in the heyday of Hammer would pass only as ironic parody today. We can see a further dissolution of borders *between* genres, making possible such hybridisations as the comedy-horror film (for example, *An American Werewolf in London* (John Landis, 1981). Within the hybrid text, two sets of narrative conventions can be discerned. They dialogically interact and comment on each other just as two contradictory modes of speech or belief systems intersect in Bakhtin's 'hybrid construction', revealing another consciousness behind that of the recognised speaker.[2] *Alien* and *Aliens* represent two 'hybrid' texts. Their relationship with each other, and with the subsequent entries in the *Alien* canon, will be examined here.

In its evolution from surprise horror hit to durable franchise, the *Alien* saga has demonstrated the quality of 'unfinalizability' that Bakhtin identifies in the dialogic word; that is, the capacity to remain semantically open, to project meaning outwards from the text and to resist the imposition of ultimate closure.[3] Apparently indestructible, the series could be said to have emulated the organism that is its main attraction, a devastatingly efficient killing machine which shows a phenomenal ability to adapt to shifting environments and whose only concern is to perpetuate itself. This adaptability means that the species can take a variety of forms, from the huge, humanoid creature of the first film, to the smaller, faster, animal-like specimen of *Alien3*. There is also a blurring of inter-species boundaries in the series: in *Alien: Resurrection* the genetic characteristics of the alien are combined with Ripley's human ones, producing a series of aborted mutants and one super-powered Ripley clone. The parallels between the way the alien species propagates itself and the way the *Alien* franchise adapts to a changing marketplace have not gone unnoticed. Michael Eaton comments that '[i]n its necessary impulse to remake itself every few years the *Alien* series must continually plunder other genres, other modes of story organisation. It must itself embark upon a process of hybridisation.'[4] It is with this process of hybridisation, the manner in which the films combine science fiction motifs with those from other genres and filmmaking traditions that this chapter is concerned. The intention is to explore the notion of *generic* hybridisation, in order to determine how the evolutionary principle of 'the survival of the fittest' is translated into 'the survival of the film with the biggest explosions and best special effects' in popular Hollywood cinema.

The late 1970s was the beginning of the era of the 'event' movie, when studios, encouraged by the success of *Jaws* (Steven Spielberg, 1975), *Star Wars* (George Lucas, 1977) and *Close Encounters of the Third Kind* (Steven Spielberg, 1977), began to embrace the ethos of the mega-budget, endlessly merchandisable genre film. Pictures of this kind, as Larry Gross points out, became 'a central economic fact, structuring all life, thought and practice in Hollywood'.[5] One of the knock-on effects of this process was that the horror and science fiction genres, which had traditionally targeted exactly the same predominantly male teenage demographic as the new breed of blockbusters, enjoyed a renaissance. *Jaws* and *Star Wars* exploited the traditions of these two genres with unprecedented success, and directors like John Carpenter produced genre films of remarkable quality. *Alien* creators Dan O'Bannon's and Ronald Shusett's idea of a deep space mining vessel menaced by an unwarranted visitor – basically 'a science-fiction version of *Jaws*' as producer Walter Hill put it[6] – represented a timely combination.

The opening sequence of *Alien* perfectly illustrates its cross-fertilisation of genres. After the credits (the letters of the title construct themselves in fractions, connoting both the growth of an organism and the tantalising visual presentation of the alien throughout the film), the first image we see is the spaceship *Nostromo*. This 'commercial towing vehicle' and its cargo, a hulking refinery with four Gothic towers, are presented in the visual iconography of horror, evoking what Harvey R. Greenberg refers to as 'some indeterminate fantasy realm – Oz, or more pointedly, the terrible dark houses of vintage horror cinema: Dr. Frankenstein's mountain laboratory, Dracula's eyrie, even the Bates's Victorian mansion'.[7]

The first cut takes us underneath the hull of the craft, whose immensity as it passes over seems an overt reference to the famous opening shot of *Star Wars*. Another cut, and we are in the bowels of the ship. A smooth tracking shot, perhaps inspired by the disturbingly subjective camera work of *Halloween* (John Carpenter, 1978), takes us through dimly lit and deserted corridors whose design refutes the antiseptic vision of space travel in *2001: A Space Odyssey* (Stanley Kubrick, 1968). But there is something more menacing about the interiors of the *Nostromo* than a bit of industrial wear and tear: they have a certain organic, anatomical quality, augmented by the womb-like pods from which the crew emerge (awoken from hypersleep by ship's computer 'Mother') and paralleled by the extraordinarily sexualised design of the derelict alien craft discovered later in the film. The *Nostromo*, despite (or perhaps because of) its functional drabness, has a living malevolence about it, a malevolence underlined when Mother, the consciousness of the craft (and spokesperson for the sinister 'Company'), is revealed to be distinctly lacking in good parenting skills. Mother's ultimate betrayal of her human charges is her rerouting of the ship to answer the signal emanating from planet LV-426. But her Company-sanctioned mission to bring back the specimen for the 'biological weapons division' is foiled by Ripley. Mother later tries to gain revenge by detonating the self-destruct mechanism of the ship, despite Ripley's attempts to override the system. This idea of a physical environment becoming sentient and turning against the protagonists is a recurrent one in horror narratives, from the grasping hands emerging from the walls in Roman Polanski's *Repulsion* (1965) to the possessed houses of *The Amityville Horror* (Stuart Rosenberg, 1979) and *Poltergeist* (Tobe Hooper, 1982).

Another narrative motif clearly imported from the horror genre is embodied in the character of Ripley, who becomes the last survivor of the *Nostromo* and ultimately destroys the predatory 'xenomorph'. Jeffrey A. Brown points out that Ripley's ability to outlive her ranking superior Dallas and the physically hulking Parker, as well as two other male crew members Brett and Kane, marks her out as an example of the staple of horror typology referred to by Carol Clover as the 'Final Girl'.[8] An archetypal protagonist of 'slasher' films such as *Halloween* and *Prom Night* (Paul Lynch, 1980), who endures into the current wave of 'postmodern' horror such as *Scream* (Wes Craven, 1997), the 'Final Girl' shows a resourcefulness and presence of mind inaccessible to other female victims, and traditionally lasts longer than the men who arrogantly assign themselves the role of protector.

Related to this aspect of Ripley's character is the fact that those who die in *Alien* seem to do so as punishment for some deviant or unsatisfactory facet of their personality – another recognisable trait of the horror film. Kane becomes the host for the 'chestburster' embryo because he transgresses the boundary between the two species by peering into the alien egg. Brett dies (in a scene masterfully handled by the film-makers, especially in terms of suspense created by editing) because he is not careful enough in looking for the ship's cat. Dallas is punished for his lacklustre leadership and his insistence that Kane should be brought onto the ship in disregard of quarantine procedures. Lambert's death is caused by her timidity, and Parker's by his belligerence and uncontrolled rage. The android Ash is destroyed by his crew mates when he turns on them. Only Ripley, who is prepared initially to sacrifice Kane to ensure the safety of the entire crew, and who shows the greatest command of the situation when the alien begins its genetically programmed killing spree, is entirely without blemish. In the logic of the horror film, this ensures her survival.

Alien did tremendous business for Twentieth Century Fox, buoyed up by the repeat audiences that had begun to attend the more notorious end of the horror market since the release of *Psycho* (Alfred Hitchcock, 1960) and had flourished with movies like *The Exorcist* (William Friedkin, 1973). James Cameron, whose blockbuster sci-fi credentials had been established with *The Terminator* in 1984, was handed the responsibility of perpetuating the saga. Interestingly, Cameron cut his directorial teeth on another sequel, *Piranha II: Flying Killers* (1981), which, like its predecessor, borrowed its premise from *Jaws*, one of the more obvious models for the first *Alien* film. *Aliens*, however, moved away from that milieu, all but jettisoning the horror strand of *Alien* for a narrative mode that resembles such war epics as *The Dirty Dozen* (Robert Aldrich, 1967) relocated to the far-flung reaches of the galaxy. *Aliens* wears this intention on its sleeve, drawing attention to its own generic composition with the knowing slogan 'This Time It's War'.

The film picks up where *Alien* left off, in setting but not in temporal terms. Ripley, still drifting in the shuttle craft in which she escaped from the *Nostromo*, is picked up by a deep space salvage crew. A representative of the Company, Carter Burke, informs a recuperating Ripley that a malfunction in the flight programme of the shuttle has caused her to remain in deep space (perfectly preserved in hypersleep) for fifty-seven years. Not much has changed on earth, however – the Company still appears to dominate global interests, and Ripley faces a disciplinary hearing where she attempts to convince her sceptical employers about the fate of the *Nostromo* and its crew. Here Ripley learns that planet LV-426, the point of origin of the original distress signal answered by the *Nostromo*, has been colonised, engineers having been sent out there decades before to establish favourable atmospheric conditions for further settlers. Ripley's worst fears are realised when Burke tells her shortly afterwards that earth has lost contact with the colony. She is persuaded to join a military rescue mission to LV-426.

Enter the war film. From the moment the crew of the *Sulako* are awoken from hypersleep and Sergeant Apone reaches for his cigar, we recognise that the signifiers and narrative conventions of the war movie are going to be added to the science fiction framework of the film. However, this being the future, there are important differences, the principal among these being the presence of several women among the Marine Corps combat unit. Indeed one female recruit, Vasquez, is quickly established as the toughest and most bloodthirsty of the lot. It is in the portrayal of this ensemble that the film particularly exhibits the influence of the war film. The troops are a classically diverse collection, comprising a host of archetypical figures: the cigar-chomping, big-hearted Apone; his nervy, ineffectual college-boy superior Gorman; the silent, stoical Hicks; the outwardly brash, inwardly cowardly Hudson; the formidable, explosive Vasquez and so on. Referred to as 'grunts' by a self-deprecating Hicks, these Marines come from a stock of characters that we have seen many times before in American cinema, notwithstanding the progressive attitude to gender. The inexperienced Gorman, for instance, is highly reminiscent of the fresh-faced Lieutenant DeBuin, whose eyes are opened by Burt Lancaster's wizened army scout in Robert Aldrich's *Ulzana's Raid* (1972).

However, it is the civilian Ripley who emerges as the figurehead of the depleted rescue team. *Aliens*, for all its conceptual simplicity and gung-ho ideology (Amy Taubin regards the film as 'the most politically conservative of the series'),[9] does interesting things with Ripley's character, bringing her to the forefront of the picture and underwriting her transition from resourceful survivor of the *Nostromo* to fully-formed action heroine. Often cited as a model for Ripley's action persona is the character Rambo, played by Sylvester Stallone in the film *First Blood* (Ted Kotcheff, 1982) and two sequels. Compounding the association is the fact that *Rambo: First Blood Part II* was written by James Cameron. As Jeffrey A. Brown notes, the visual image of Cameron's Ripley differs from the familiar Rambo iconography only in one detail: whereas publicity photographs of Stallone's character routinely showed him carrying a prisoner of war, Ripley is often depicted with the little girl Newt in her arms.[10] Rambo, the quintessential muscles-for-brains action hero, is transformed into a caring, sharing action heroine. It is a calculated remaking of Ripley.

Perhaps the most commented on of *Aliens'* extensions to Ripley's character is her relationship with Newt, the last survivor of the colony on LV-426. Newt appears to bring out in Ripley a maternal instinct that feeds into the series' discourse on reproduction. However, Cameron's original conception was more complex. In footage shot for *Aliens* but never theatrically released (surfacing instead on a 'Special Edition' video release in 1992), Ripley is told of the fate of her own daughter, never mentioned elsewhere in the series, who has died aged seventy-six during Ripley's deep space slumber. The restoration of this crucial narrative material makes the 'Special Edition' of *Aliens* a very different picture from the cinematically released incarnation. Regrettably, the most recent re-release of *Aliens* (a digitally remastered video version in 1997) elects once again to omit this strand of sub-plot, shutting the narrative door on Ripley's daughter and all the resonances that are associated with her.

Echoes of the war film are everywhere in *Aliens*, from the Vietnam-style graffiti emblazoned on the Marines' helmets and

weapons, to the military parlance that is their mode of com-
munication. The film presents an essentially twentieth-century
conception of warfare, filtered through dozens of war movies
and enhanced with the awesome hardware that is a
prerequisite of the sci-fi genre. Gateway Space Station, the
various spacecrafts featured, and above all the intricately
detailed weaponry are lovingly photographed by Cameron.
Arguably the closest thing to an erotic moment in the film
occurs when Hicks instructs Ripley on how to handle a 'close
personal friend', his trusty pulse rifle (with added grenade
launcher). Ripley learns rapidly – she is soon seen strapping
two huge weapons together and equipping herself with
ammunition and grenades, to the accompaniment of military
style drums. (James Horner's score, with its reliance on martial
sounding brass and percussion, is another important factor in
the construction of the film as war epic.) A scene where the
surviving Marines, Ripley and Burke, plan their defence over
a blueprint of the complex is redolent of the 'last stand' being
prepared in any number of cinematic war rooms. However, the
film's treatment of the Marines' alien adversaries dilutes the
complexity that *Alien* had striven for. They become 'monsters',
a viewpoint legitimised by the childish perspective of Newt,
and are fit only to be blown away. By attaching the label of
'evil' to the aliens, the film risks losing the layer of irony
surrounding the real reason behind the mission: the
Company's desire to protect its colonial interests (although
Ripley does memorably compare the treacherous Burke to the
aliens – 'you don't see them fucking each other over for a
goddamn percentage').

By the time the cycle reaches its third instalment, the cor-
respondences between the amorphous genetic properties of the
xenomorph and the necessarily fluid character of its parent
franchise are explicit. Harvey R. Greenberg notes that, in
audience responses to the first film, 'awareness of [the alien's]
quick change potential keeps the viewer in a state of even
greater unease, anticipating what chimerical composition the
creature will choose in its next reincarnation'.[11] This sense of
anticipation seemed evident in the way that audiences waited
for the next episode; what 'chimerical composition' of genre
and narrative form would the next mutation take?

The thought that the series should remake itself once again had obviously struck Twentieth Century Fox too. In a move that could be viewed as either admirable or reckless, the studio backed a script that, while respectful of the horror heritage of *Alien*, was quite unlike either of the first two films. It underlined this fact by killing off Hicks and Newt, two of the most popular characters in *Aliens*, before the credits had rolled. To bring this dark tale to the screen, the studio selected David Fincher, a director of pop music promos with a highly developed visual sense, but no experience of the demands of features. Fincher's inexperience shows not so much in how the film is presented – it is visually impressive – as in the way that the narrative lacks either the dreadful inevitability of *Alien* or the textbook build-up of *Aliens*. The movie aims for something more than the inspired reworkings of established genres that constitute the first two films, but fails precisely because of the absence of a firm generic framework. *Alien3* is far richer conceptually than the second episode: it returns to the psycho-sexual paranoia of the first film and, as Amy Taubin points out, introduces a new metaphor equating the alien with the Aids virus.[12] Yet it is only fleetingly faithful to the audience-pleasing principles on which *Alien*, for all its undoubted sub-textual riches, was founded. Taubin may be exaggerating when she declares that *Alien3* leans towards the avant-garde, but it certainly moves too far from the safety net of a recognisable genre to connect with its target audience.[13] The first two films do not disregard or bypass genre in this way, but rather twist it to their own narrative ends.

One of the factors behind this problem is how little the conventions of science fiction play a part in the film. Despite their narrative affiliations with the traditionally terrestrial genres of horror and the war film, *Alien* and *Aliens* make the most of their unearthly settings, albeit using them in a context that is more realistic than fantastic. The android Ash, the *Nostromo*, the alien vessel and the strange world on which it is discovered all contribute to the futuristic iconography of the first film. This is taken even further with the fetishistic hardware and technology of *Aliens* (most memorably in the cargo-loader exoskeleton that Ripley dons to slug it out with the alien queen). Fincher's film, by contrast, has precious few scenes of space travel, and even less hi-tech weaponry. The Fury 161 prison complex looks more like a Victorian mental institution than a futuristic space colony. The plot dictates that the film should be shorn of virtually all science fiction para-phernalia: the prison is devoid of all technology, while its inmates are devoted to a quasi-luddite 'apocalyptic, millennarian, fundamentalist' variation of Christianity. Fury 161 is a fairly well-realised, threatening environment for the action. Amy Taubin argues that its purpose is to represent a primal locus of cinematic and psychological fear, redolent of 'every prison, shiphold, sewer, grave robbing, morgue, con-centration camp, New York subway, lunatic asylum movie you've ever seen ... whatever images surface on your dream screen'.[14] However, Fury 161 evokes so many other apocalyptic scenarios that it has no real identity of its own. The abandoned industrial vestiges of the refinery hint at the *Nostromo*, but Fury 161 evokes neither the *Nostromo*'s sense of claustrophobia, nor the uninhabited desolation of the colonial outpost in *Aliens*.

Even the alien creature in Fincher's film is less threatening. The film makes a basic error of narrative judgement in assuming that a lone organism could once again terrify an audience that still had the image of the immense army of *Aliens* etched into its memory. The tag-line used to sell the film ('The Bitch is Back') plays on Ripley's reference to the alien queen as 'bitch' in *Aliens*, but here it signifies the indomitable Ripley as much as her adversary. The principle behind Fincher's presentation of the alien is to shock the audience. Only the death of the first inmate utilises suspense effectively: the hapless Murphy hears an animal noise and, mistaking the xenomorph for his pet dog, peers into a dark corner to investigate. We are given little or no warning of impending doom in most of the other death scenes. (This contrasts with Scott's method in *Alien*, which, in deference to classical horror practice, seeks to draw out the suspense.) Clemens (Charles Dance) is decapitated when the creature emerges behind a curtain in the medical bay, and shortly afterwards his superior Andrews (Brian Glover) suffers the same fate and is yanked into an overhead air duct. There is some thrilling subjective camerawork from the point-of-view of the alien as it races through a labyrinthine system of tunnels in pursuit of its prey. However, *Alien* is far more effective in building up an aura of predatory invincibility around the creature.

Alien3 can only be considered a failure if it is measured by the high standards set by its predecessors. And these are not just standards of 'quality'; there are very specific narrative 'rules' that the third episode does not observe. The first two *Alien* films, although very differently executed, led audiences to expect certain things from the franchise – suspense, terror, action, eye-popping special effects, gore, futuristic design and serious sci-fi hardware. These were in short supply in the darker, more downbeat third film. The more ambitious *Alien3* should be commended for refusing to repeat the formula of Cameron's box-office champion. It remains an interesting example of what happens when a sequel dares to distance itself from its heritage. Fincher's dystopic vision would be realised in a more appropriate generic context in his next film, *Se7en* (1995), of which the cheerless urban setting and pessimistic tone owes much to *Alien3*.

The role of Sigourney Weaver in the production of the *Alien* films had increased with the third instalment, where she received a co-producer's credit and contributed to the writing of the screenplay.[15] Another episode without her participation was unthinkable, and Ripley's swan dive into a fiery death at the end of *Alien3* suggested that the cycle of films was also at an end. It is uncertain whether the eventual production of *Alien: Resurrection* was purely motivated by a desire to rekindle the profit-making momentum of the first two films, or by a nobler artistic purpose; but the former seems more likely. The task of commercial resurrection was entrusted to Frenchman Jean-Pierre Jeunet, one half (along with Marc Caro) of the team behind the arthouse hits *Delicatessen* (1991) and *The City of Lost Children* (1995). Those films had displayed a highly distinctive visual style, making Jeunet a natural contender for the *Alien* series. Jeunet was not the studio's first choice of director – Danny Boyle and even James Cameron were among those said to have turned down the project. But the engagement of a director with European arthouse sensibilities suggested that Fox wanted to emphasise the high quality of the franchise (and perhaps its status as a training ground for successful directors) while simultaneously reinvigorating its marketability.

Joss Whedon, the screenwriter of *Alien: Resurrection*, approached the apparent dead end of *Alien3* as an opportunity to weave together the reproductive discourse running through the series with developments in contemporary science. Two centuries after Ripley's death, unscrupulous military research scientists attempt to recreate the alien species from Ripley's genetic material. Clone number eight (Weaver) is a by-product of this process, her enhanced physical powers suggesting that she represents a genetic amalgamation of alien and human. When the reconstructed aliens escape from their containment units on the space vessel *Auriga*, Ripley teams up with a band of space pirates (unwitting accomplices in the sinister experiment) to destroy the creatures. The fact that a fail-safe mechanism on the craft has re-routed it to earth makes this task all the more imperative.

Alien: Resurrection represents something of a fusion itself, marrying the no-nonsense narrative ethos and conventional sci-fi trimmings of *Aliens* with the dark tone of *Alien3*. Enthralling set-pieces abound (notably the underwater scenes, where Ripley and the others have to evade their adversaries by swimming through a flooded kitchen area), and the visual presentation of the aliens is enhanced by the use of computer-generated effects, but the reconstruction of Ripley that is the fulcrum of the narrative is distinctly ambiguous. This ambiguity is movingly realised in a scene where Ripley discovers the aborted monstrosities that represent the first seven attempts to reconstitute the xenomorph. No longer threatened by the aliens whom she now equals in physical ability, the new model Ripley has her loyalties tested by the stand-off between her dual progenitors. Her decision to side with the pirates seems to be influenced by an emotional attachment to Call (Winona Ryder). Call is subsequently revealed to be an android, aligning her character with the benign android Bishop of *Aliens*. As Michael Eaton observes, one trope of the series appears to be the displacement of 'individuated characteristics' onto non-human protagonists; the space pirates, like the ineffectual Marines in *Aliens*, 'merely panic and swear and run around a lot',[16] leaving the defence of their species to Ripley and Call. There is some reference to the discourse of gender rivalry that informs *Aliens* in the character of Johner, a version of the Rambo archetype supplanted by Vasquez in Cameron's film, who is initially hostile to the effortlessly superior Ripley but becomes more admiring and smitten of this Amazonian hybrid as the narrative unfolds.

Casting and billing provide insights into the film's aspirations. In promotional material for the movie, Weaver, the recipient of top billing since *Aliens*, shares equal above-the-line status with Winona Ryder. The incorporation of Ryder into the franchise made sound commercial sense for both star and studio: Ryder is one of the top three or four young female actors in Hollywood, and consequently will always provide extra pulling-power. As far as Ryder's career is concerned, her part in the big-budget *Alien: Resurrection* was a necessary contrast to a string of roles in prestigious but unprofitable period dramas. When Ryder's involvement was first announced, followers of the series could be forgiven for imagining that she was being groomed to take on Weaver's mantle of protagonist in a further set of adventures. As it stands, both Call and the Ripley clone survive to the end credits (their return to earth signalling another possible avenue for the franchise). Elsewhere in the cast, Dominique Pinon (Vriess) and Ron Perlman (Johner) establish links with Jeunet's previous work (both actors appear in *The City of Lost Children*; Pinon is also the star of *Delicatessen*). Jeunet brings something of the visual character and black humour of both those offerings to his Hollywood debut.

At the time of the British release of *Alien: Resurrection*, a feature in the film magazine *Empire* proffered several tongue-in-cheek suggestions for a fifth movie: *Honey I Shrunk the Alien* (directed by Frank Oz), *Manhattan Monster Mystery* (directed by Woody Allen), *A Room With A Crew* (a Merchant/Ivory production), and so on.[17] This indicates how far 'generic hybridisation' has become a characteristic of the series. All too often in Hollywood practice, formulaic sequels suggest that the franchise is an artistically redundant strategy. But the *Alien* saga has proved its capacity to reinvent itself in interesting ways again and again, and it deserves respect for trying to do something a little different each time. The secret of satisfying a genre audience, however, is not to try to do anything *too* different, as the failed experiment of *Alien3* proved. The structure of a genre is constantly changing, mutating, and every new entry ideally contributes to the ongoing 'life' of the genre and raises the stakes a little further. Using Bakhtin's term, we could say that the *Alien* series contributes to the ongoing 're-accentuation' of the science fiction genre, keeping it moving forward as a dynamically evolving narrative form by promoting interaction with other modes of textual organisation.[18] The *Alien* cycle, itself a convergence of multiple intertextual sources, has seen elements of its structure and style reworked incessantly in the science fiction genre, in films such as *Predator* (John McTiernan, 1987), *Leviathan* (George P. Cosmatos, 1989) and *Starship Troopers* (Paul Verhoeven, 1997). At one point, an *Alien Vs. Predator* franchise hybrid was even put into pre-production.[19] The influence of the series extends to other genres (Mel Brooks' comedy *Spaceballs* (1987)), and even into other media (the successful *Alien* comic book line). Even if the series is not continued beyond *Alien: Resurrection*, it will continue to inflect film-making by the processes of intertextual dialogism. As for a fifth instalment, Sigourney Weaver is apparently contemplating directing a prequel set on the home planet of the alien.[20] The perspective of a female director would certainly represent another fascinating change of course for the series.

Notes

1. Mikhail Bakhtin, 'Epic and Novel' in *The Dialogic Imagination*, ed. Michael Holquist, trans. Caryl Emerson and Michael Holquist (Austin: University of Texas Press, 1994), p. 5.
2. Mikhail Bakhtin, 'Discourse in the Novel' in *The Dialogic Imagination*, p. 304.
3. Mikhail Bakhtin, *Problems of Dostoevsky's Poetics*, ed. and trans. Caryl Emerson (Minneapolis and London: University of Minnesota Press, 1997), p. 53.
4. Michael Eaton, 'Born Again', *Sight and Sound*, 7: 12 (December 1997), p. 9.
5. Larry Gross, 'Big and Loud', *Sight and Sound*, 5: 8 (August 1995), p. 7.

6. Quoted in Gareth Grundy, 'Kill By Mouth', *Neon*, 12 (December 1997), p. 118.
7. Harvey R. Greenberg, 'Reimagining the Gargoyle: Psychoanalytic Notes on Alien', *Camera Obscura*, 15 (1986), p. 92.
8. Jeffrey A. Brown, 'Gender and the Action Heroine: Hardbodies and the Point of No Return', *Cinema Journal*, 35: 3 (Spring 1996), p. 52.
9. Amy Taubin, 'Invading Bodies: *Alien3* and the Trilogy', *Sight and Sound*, 2: 3 (July 1992), p. 9.
10. Brown, 'Gender and the Action Heroine', pp. 57–8.
11. Greenberg, 'Reimagining the Gargoyle', p. 94.
12. Taubin, 'Invading Bodies', p. 10.
13. Ibid., p. 9.
14. Ibid., p. 9.
15. Ros Jennings, 'Desire and Design: Ripley Undressed' in Tamsin Wilton (ed.), *Immortal Invisible: Lesbians and the Moving Image* (London: Routledge, 1995), p. 203.
16. Eaton, 'Born Again', p. 9.
17. Andrew Collins, 'What Alien Did Next', *Empire*, 102 (December 1997), p. 136.
18. Bakhtin, 'Discourse in the Novel', p. 417.
19. Ian Nathan, 'Alien Reincarnation', *Empire*, 102 (December 1997), p. 124.
20. Ibid., p. 136.

10

Aliens, (M)Others, Cyborgs: The Emerging Ideology of Hybridity

Patricia Linton

Aliens in recent science fiction demonstrate the ascendancy of the hybrid, the cyborg. In many contemporary fiction and film narratives, the alien is represented not as definitively other, but as an in-between creature – not entirely strange, not entirely human. Such texts focus on the consciousness of the hybrid or cyborg and the place of the deliberately constructed or engineered creature in human society. For example, one of the significant ways in which Ridley Scott's 1982 film *Blade Runner* diverges from Philip K. Dick's 1968 novel *Do Androids Dream of Electric Sheep* is its attention to the experience of the androids. As the film progresses, it is increasingly the plight of the androids, rather than the mission of the Blade Runner, that is most compelling. The android Roy Batty's fury at the shortness of his time, his impulse to confront his creator, and his surprising gesture of reconciliation as his time expires, which Deckard interprets as an overwhelming love of life, are all distinctively human preoccupations. What perhaps resonates most poignantly is Batty's sense of individual worth, his implicit argument that his life has value: 'I have seen things ... All those moments will be lost in time, like tears in rain.'

In questioning the priority of the human over other forms of existence, and particularly in challenging the aloof and indifferent creator, *Blade Runner*'s Roy Batty echoes the complaint of the creature in Mary Shelley's *Frankenstein* (1818). Similarly, other contemporary texts such as Richard Powers's 1990 novel *Galatea 2.2* and Shelley Jackson's 1995 hypertext fiction *Patchwork Girl* explore the consciousness of a creation that has been endowed with human values but knows it is not human. Each of these narratives develops its characters and its arguments via intertextual dialogue with Mary Shelley's *Frankenstein*, particularly Shelley's interrogation of what it means to be a person. This chapter examines two 1997 works, Kirsten Bakis's novel *Lives of the Monster Dogs* and the film *Alien: Resurrection*, directed by Jean-Pierre Jeunet, to demonstrate that their dialogue with *Frankenstein* illuminates changing contemporary attitudes toward hybridity, new articulations of the relationship between creature and creator and a new emphasis on female agency.

In representing hybridity, *Lives of the Monster Dogs* and *Alien: Resurrection* provide close parallels to *Frankenstein* because, unlike either *Blade Runner* or *Galatea 2.2*, they portray the alien as physically monstrous. The androids in *Blade Runner* are physically beautiful, certainly as appealing to look upon as the human characters. In *Galatea 2.2*, the alien consciousness has no body; the computer program 'Helen' is so complex that it is distributed across a number of sites throughout the university. Shelley emphasises, however, that in physical form Frankenstein's creature is shockingly grotesque. Frankenstein repeatedly comments that the body parts chosen for their proportion and beauty are in the aggregate painfully ugly; Walton, who has become sympathetic to the monster, nevertheless finds it hard to lift his eyes to look at him. The creature himself responds to his appearance with horror: 'At first I started back, unable to believe that it was indeed I who was reflected in the mirror; and when I became fully convinced that I was in reality the monster that I am, I was filled with the bitterest sensations of despondence and mortification.'[1] Many commentators, among them Peter Brook, have noted the disparity between the appearance and the voice of the creature in Shelley's novel:

> As a verbal creation, he is the very opposite of the monstrous: he is a sympathetic and persuasive participant in Western culture. All of the Monster's interlocutors – including, finally, the reader – must come to terms with this contradiction between the verbal and the visual.[2]

In Shelley's fiction, the gap between physical repulsion and intellectual kinship cannot be bridged. As Donna Haraway points out in 'A Cyborg Manifesto', 'Monsters have always defined the limits of community in Western imaginations.'[3]

Lives of the Monster Dogs and *Alien: Resurrection* raise similar tensions but resolve them differently. The monsters in Bakis's novel are 150 educated dogs, genetically and mechanically engineered to match human intelligence, walk upright with the aid of canes, speak through mechanised voice boxes and manipulate objects with prosthetic hands. Like Frankenstein's creature, the monster dogs are 'unnatural'; they are cyborg combinations of animal and machine, pathetic or disturbing in their efforts to be as human as possible. They pride themselves on maintaining erect posture, wearing elegant clothes and numbering among their cohort dogs who are composers and scientists. But like Frankenstein's creature, they know that they are monsters; they have a horror of being, or being perceived as, ordinary dogs. The political leader of the Society of Dogs, Klaue Lutz, calls himself 'an ugly mistake made by a madman'.[4] One of the most cultured dogs, the historian Ludwig von Sacher, wonders what it would be like to be human: 'I spend a great deal of time trying to imagine it. We all do, because we want to be like you, of course ... Being a dog is nothing ... It is nothing but an absence, a negative.'[5] Ludwig recounts the unhappiness of Rupert, the very first successfully functioning monster dog:

> He had spent too much of his life as an ordinary dog, and to be suddenly endowed with an understanding of what that was – what he still was, in many ways – was a great shock to him. He said later to a friend that it had been like waking up from a pleasant dream to find himself enslaved, as if he had been captured by members of another race while he slept, and taken away to their country. It is a terrible thing to be a dog and know it; and I suppose it was worse for him, because he could remember a time when he did not.[6]

Commenting on the history of the dogs after their revolution against their human masters, in which they massacred all humans in the city of Rankstadt, Ludwig remarks, 'We have money now, perhaps we are not slaves, but we are still monsters.'[7]

The monster dogs' pride in their 'humanity' is so strong that they prefer to die rather than to lose their cyborg identities. When a mysterious mental illness causes almost all of the dogs to begin to revert to canine consciousness and behaviour, they isolate themselves from humans and make what amounts to a suicide pact in order to avoid humiliation or exploitation by humans. Lydia Petze, the only monster dog who will actually survive, tells her human friend Cleo Pira: 'It's a way to end the sickness with dignity. It makes sense to us. Since we're all in the castle, no one outside needs to know.' To Cleo's objection that the dogs who carry out the plan are murderers, Lydia replies, 'It isn't murder if the victim has agreed to it.'[8]

In Bakis's novel, the horror of the alien (that is, the non-human) is felt more powerfully by the dogs themselves than by humans inside or outside of the fiction. As Theodore Ziolkowski has demonstrated, the talking dog has a long history in literature.[9] The close association between dogs and humans, amplified by the literary motif of the philosophical dog, makes it more likely that the monster dogs will strike the reader as fascinating and perverse than as truly disgusting. In fact, the idea of the monster dogs may seem less grotesque than the representation of a reanimated human composed of fragments of dead bodies. While the monster dogs are more explicitly other than android aliens like those in *Blade Runner*, what is truly disturbing is the instability of their enlightened state. Indeed, the fact that the dogs value clarity of mind and personal dignity more than life strengthens rather than diminishes their kinship with humankind. The objective of Cleo Pira's narrative is to commemorate the lives of the dogs and preserve their stories; in her preface, she thanks Lydia, the lone survivor, for her 'sustaining friendship'.[10]

In the sequence of *Alien* films, on the other hand, the resources of the film medium make it possible to convey far more forcefully a visceral sense that the alien is horrific. In this ongoing narrative, the enemy beings encountered by human space travellers are highly intelligent, but monstrous in size and shape; they have giant, slimy, insect-like bodies with yellowish-green acid blood. They need living creatures to incubate and feed their developing larvae, and humans are apparently their only available prey. In the extended narrative that now comprises four films, it is the mission of all the admirable humans, particularly Ellen Ripley (Sigourney Weaver), to prevent this alien race from reaching earth.[11] Ripley's own horror of the aliens and her recognition of their menace is so strong that in the third film she commits suicide to prevent the birth of the alien queen implanted within her.

In *Alien: Resurrection*, the fourth film in the series, the horror of the alien is reinforced in a variety of ways. Most obvious is the distressingly graphic depiction of the aliens as gruesome predators. But more interesting is the positioning of the two main characters, Ripley and Call (Winona Ryder) as aliens. Halfway through the film, Call is revealed as an android. At that point, Call's surviving shipmates (all males) express contempt for her, in spite of the fact that they owe her their lives, and particular distaste for the fact that they had desired her sexually. Their altered attitude is reinforced by the loathing Call expresses toward herself. To Ripley, a hybrid human/alien clone, Call says, 'At least there's part of you that's human … I'm disgusting.'

The identity of Ripley has been ambiguous, for both characters and viewers, almost from the beginning of the film. Although of course she looks like the human hero of the previous films, her status as other is constantly reinforced. Her blood is red but acidic enough to corrode metal. She speaks scathingly of herself as not alive, not real; when asked how she dealt with the aliens in their last confrontation, she says sardonically, 'I died.' In her first encounter with Call, Ripley expresses in gesture and dialogue her partial identification with the alien. In this scene, she does not stand fully upright, and she moves in a sinuous, snake-like manner. At one point, she cups Call's face in her hands, the first two fingers of each hand extended and curved in imitation of the claw-like appendages on the limbs of the alien creatures. As Call tries to learn where on the spaceship the alien is housed, she implies Ripley's complicity with the alien queen: 'You're a thing, a construct. They brought it out of you.' Ripley replies, 'Not all the way out … I can feel it behind my eyes. I can hear it moving.' Thereafter,

Call warns her shipmates against trusting Ripley: 'She is not human, and she's too much of a risk.'

The initial turning point in the relationship between Call and Ripley occurs when Ripley confronts earlier avatars of herself – seven clones preserved in a laboratory, their bodies shockingly grotesque combinations of human and alien components, rejected by the scientists who created them not because they were inhuman but because they were inadequate recreations of the alien queen. Most disturbing, one is alive, bound to a table, sustained by mechanical life support. In a painful, rasping whisper she begs Ripley to kill her, and at Call's urging Ripley does so. The scene establishes beyond question Ripley's hybridity. Ripley is not a human detached from an alien but a creature with mixed human and alien genes whose surface happens to appear comfortingly human. Although she is organic, she is in Haraway's terms a cyborg, a monster.

Writing about feminist science fiction, Haraway comments that cyborgs 'make very problematic the statuses of man or woman, human, artefact, member of a race, individual entity, or body'.[12] Four characters in *Alien: Resurrection* survive the human/alien confrontation on the research station and escape to earth; all are in some sense hybrids or cyborgs. Ripley is a human/alien hybrid, and Call is a machine invested with the most admirable aspects of human character – when Ripley discovers that Call is not organic, she comments, 'I should have known. No human being is so humane.' In addition to Ripley and Call, the survivors include Vriess (Dominique Pinon), a human with disabled legs whose wheelchair makes him a human/machine entity, and Johner (Ron Perlman), a human whose size and unusual facial contours – as well as the iconography established in previous roles – gesture toward human/animal identity.[13] It is hardly surprising, in a film of this genre, that few characters remain alive at the end, but there is nothing in the formula of the genre that points to these two as the humans most likely to survive; they are not the best looking, nor the most sympathetic, nor the most essential to the mission (neither of them, for example, knows how to pilot the escape ship). Part of the message of this film, however, is that survival of the fittest favours the cyborg.

Both *Lives of the Monster Dogs* and *Alien: Resurrection* echo, with a difference, the vexed relationship between creator and creature in Mary Shelley's *Frankenstein*. In Bakis's novel, the dogs are obsessed with their designer, a Prussian scientist named Augustus Rank; they consider Rank their creator, although the plans for a race of monster dogs that he developed in 1882 were not successfully implemented until 1968. The dogs believe that they are sustained by the spirit of their creator, and that the loss of his spirit has precipitated the illness afflicting them. *Lives of the Monster Dogs* has a layered narrative structure clearly modelled on Shelley's text. The original novel opens with the letters of Robert Walton to his sister; embedded within that narrative is Frankenstein's narrative to Walton, and within Frankenstein's tale, the narrative of the creature to his maker. Bakis opens with the account of the monster dogs by Cleo Pira, who presents herself as a human observer of the final events and editor of the papers of the monster historian, Ludwig von Sacher, whose papers form the bulk of the text. Cleo's narrative is dated 2017; most of Ludwig's papers are transcribed by him in 2010. Embedded within Ludwig's chronicle are scattered fragments of Rank's journal, which date from the late 1800s. Thus, although both novels are framed by the narration of a witness, the delivery of the two inner narratives is reversed. In Bakis's tale, the account of the creator is inaccessible, except in bits and pieces.

In both novels, the human condition is mirrored in the relationship between the creator and the monstrous creature. However, while Frankenstein's creature accuses his creator of being a bad parent, refusing to nurture his offspring, Ludwig portrays the dogs as bad children, doomed because they have lost contact with their spiritual father. Part of the final entry in Rank's diary states: 'Had I completed my dogs, their love would have been fierce and undying ... Someday they will be created and they will know that they were everything to me, that I loved them like my children, that I loved them before they existed. They will wait for my return as dogs wait for their masters ...' Both the loving, immortal parent and the wilful, rebellious children are endangered by the children's loss of faith in the vision of the father and his promise to return to them. Ludwig believes that the dogs are regressing because they are no longer nurtured by Rank's spirit: 'I believe these memory lapses are connected to the disappearance of Rank's spirit. I believe my consciousness is disintegrating, just as his consciousness is.'[14]

But it is clear from the history Ludwig constructs that the dogs' father/god is a monster. Augustus Rank was an emotionally stunted person who 'discovered his passion for dismembering living creatures' at the age of eleven, three months after his mother died and his father abandoned him to indifferent relatives.[15] As a young man, he slit the throat of his half-brother, his rival for the hand of a woman who had rejected him. Already a cocaine addict in early adulthood, Rank began to envision applications for his macabre experiments and was eventually commissioned by Wilhelm II of Germany to create an invincible army of intelligent dogs. Ultimately, he fled to Canada as the leader of a cult of reclusive scientists, sustained by funds embezzled from his patron and still determined to engineer the world's strongest army, which he himself would command. In one of the fragments of his diary preserved among Ludwig's papers, Rank writes: 'When I am done I won't need the people anymore. The dogs will be my people, perfect extensions of my will ... They will be absolutely obedient to me. Their minds will be my mind, their hearts will be mine, their teeth will be my teeth, their hands will be my hands ...'[16] Rank is a mad god, but without him the dogs have no reason to exist, no destiny. Ludwig understands that Rank was a person incapable of human love and compassion, but he also knows that a sense of higher purpose, the expectation that their creator will come again to lead the dogs to some undefined victory, is necessary to sustain them. If god is dead, the dogs are condemned, collectively and individually, to psychic loneliness. Ludwig writes: 'Once we were no more than an idea in his mind, a desire in his heart. Then we were all together in him and there was no loneliness. There was no difference between master and dog. But I cannot remember what that was like.'[17] If the metaphorical implication of Shelley's novel is that god is a self-absorbed and indifferent father, the implication in *Lives of the Monster Dogs* is that both the father/creator and his creatures are grotesques.

In *Alien: Resurrection*, as well, the father/creator is portrayed as monstrous. But from the opening moments of the film an important distinction is made between fathers and mothers. The narrative begins with a voiceover by Ripley: 'My mommy always said there were no monsters, no real ones, but there are.' The next image is the group of male scientists hovering around Ripley's unconscious body, preparing to remove the alien foetus from her chest. The juxtaposition suggests that these men are real monsters, an implication reinforced by their initial indecision about whether Ripley herself is interesting enough to keep once the alien has been extracted. In this narrative, fathers are engineers and disciplinarians. The male scientists train Ripley to speak and to modify her aggressive behaviour; they attempt to train the alien species in the same manner – punishing disobedience and rewarding acquiescence to the master's will. Representing metonymically the culture of the research station, the computer system that operates the vessel is nicknamed 'father'. When Call connects her own circuitry to the master computer in order to open an escape route for the human party, one of the directors of the lab, Dr Wren (J.E. Freeman), instructs 'father' to locate the power drain, to which Call retorts, 'Father's dead, asshole.'

As in the other Alien films, the most important characters in *Alien: Resurrection* are females: Ripley, Call, the alien queen. All are, in the broadest sense, mothers. Call is programmed to nurture and protect humans. Although Ripley is an unwilling vessel who, in an earlier incarnation, killed herself to avoid motherhood, she consistently identifies herself as the mother of the alien queen. When Call is attempting to locate the queen, she asks Ripley, 'Where is it?' and Ripley responds bitterly, 'You mean, my "baby"?' When other members of the human supply party want to know who she is, Ripley says, 'I'm the monster's mother.' She has a psychic bond with the alien queen that enables her to sense its location and its physical condition; she knows when the queen is in pain and about to give birth. (The cloned queen is also a hybrid, and according to one of the research scientists, Ripley's genetic gift to her is a human reproductive system.) At some level, in spite of Ripley's 'human' resistance, the psychic connection is compelling. When Ripley pauses at a hatch and then plunges down into the birthing chamber, she lies in the coils of the queen's appendages, in what appears to be a mutual embrace.

The issues associated with Ripley's 'motherhood' are complex and intersect in telling ways with problems posed in *Frankenstein*. Essentially, Frankenstein's creature argues that the man who created him has a responsibility to be his parent. This, according to Ellen Moers, is the component of Shelley's novel that is 'most interesting, most powerful, and most feminine: ... the motif of revulsion against newborn life, and the drama of guilt, dread, and flight surrounding birth and its consequences'.[18] Ripley is not the creator of the alien queen, nor of the queen's infant daughter; the use of her body to recreate the queen is more akin to rape than to any other human act. While Ripley experiences an emotional bond with the queen, the alien is not a being that seeks the kind of mothering humans know how to give. However, with the next generation of alien offspring, Ripley's relationship with her alien progeny alters, and her emotional dilemma becomes more acute. As Ripley looks on, the alien queen delivers an infant who looks neither human nor alien; indeed, more than anything else, the monster baby resembles one of the early clones preserved in the research laboratory – humanoid rather than insect-like, but with poorly defined facial features and misshapen body contours. Physically competent immediately after her birth, the infant gazes at the two creatures closest to her and 'chooses' Ripley as her 'mother'. The huge baby lops off the head of the alien queen, devours a human cocooned by the queen to provide nourishment for her brood (the human victim is one of the scientist/creators, who richly deserves his fate), and pursues Ripley to the escape ship.

In Moers's words, *Frankenstein* is 'Mary Shelley's fantasy of the newborn as at once monstrous agent of destruction and piteous victim of parental abandonment'.[19] In *Alien: Resurrection*, the alien queen's doubly hybrid daughter is at once a ravening beast and a mewling infant who wants to be mothered. Ripley, in effect, must choose whom to nurture. She enters the hold of the escape ship to find that the creature has dispatched another hapless crew member and is menacing Call. Before consigning the predatory baby to the emptiness of space, however, Ripley caresses her face in a lingering embrace.

As the creature's body is sucked out into space, Ripley and the monster child reach out toward one another in ambiguous reciprocal gestures that appear to be partly a leave-taking, partly a mutual appeal, and partly an involuntary effect of the space-draught that is pulling everything in the hold of the ship toward the void. Thus, Ripley repeats Frankenstein's abandonment of a monster who has no other parent, an abandonment that is in this case almost literally an abortion.

Neither *Lives of the Monster Dogs* nor *Alien: Resurrection* portrays females as creators, but both emphasise female agency and the sustaining power of bonds between adult women. In representing female aliens as more formidable than males, these texts reiterate norms of science fiction extending back at least to *Frankenstein*. Robin Roberts argues that female aliens in traditional science fiction embody the male fear of 'femininity as magical, reproductive, dangerous, and threatening to men'.[20] Thus Frankenstein cannot finally bring himself to create a mate for his monster, although he is moved by the loneliness of the creature who, without the care of a parent or the friendship of humans, is bereft of all companionship. Frankenstein 'tears to pieces' the partially formed female he has constructed, arguing that he cannot risk the possibility of a race of monsters: 'one of the first results of those sympathies for which the daemon thirsted would be children, and a race of devils would be propagated upon the earth, who might make the very existence of the species of man a condition precarious and full of terror'.[21] Even recognising the equity of the creature's demand for a mate – a request that echoes Adam's plea to God for a companion – Frankenstein cannot bring himself to act the part of the creator once again, and he sees his refusal as a defence of humankind. Roberts notes that depictions of female aliens in popular fiction are 'cast in the image of Frankenstein's monster's mate as well as in the image of mythical female creatures such as the witch or the Medusa'. Female aliens represent the 'uncontrollable feminine' and offer 'an alternative to science through their bodies'.[22]

What is particularly interesting in the texts discussed here is that female agency is more effective and more dangerous than male agency, even when reproductive power is not the issue. The monster dogs cannot reproduce themselves – that is, they do not know how to replicate the genetic and surgical manipulations that produce their enhanced abilities, nor do they understand the design of the prosthetic devices that enable them to speak and to manipulate objects with artificial hands. Nevertheless, the Samoyed Lydia Petze, the only female monster who figures significantly in the story, surpasses the males physically, emotionally and ethically. She is capable enough as a fighter to kill Klaue Lutz when he tries to assassinate Cleo. She acknowledges feeling the blood lust natural to dogs, yet even in moments of intense emotion, she is able to subordinate that instinct to moral and intellectual judgements. When asked why she did not participate in the massacre of humans that was the culmination of the dogs' revolution, she answers, 'Because I felt it was wrong ... that's all.'[23] She is the only one of the monster dogs to escape the mysterious deterioration that afflicts all others of her kind.

In the *Alien* films, the alien species resembles an insect colony; not only is the queen larger and more powerful than male soldiers or drones, it is she who is central to the social organisation and the reproductive success of the colony. Sigourney Weaver's Ripley, the only continuing human character, survives because she is smarter, stronger, more committed than her confreres; in the first three films, the significant contest is between two females – Ripley and the alien queen. In *Alien: Resurrection*, the physical and mental prowess of the hybrid Ripley has increased exponentially. She beats human males at basketball and tosses them about like mannequins; she has acquired a kind of extra-sensory perception that enables her to read both aliens and humans. As portrayed in this film, Ripley is not the object of a sexual gaze on the part of either the characters or the camera. Her costuming and her mannerisms represent her as virtually androgynous. Call, who is not human, appears more con-ventionally feminine, but it becomes clear that her agency has nothing to do with sexual or reproductive power. She is not only more resilient but more sensitive and compassionate than ordinary humans because she is literally well built, programmed to assimilate data that humans miss and to survive assaults that the human body cannot withstand. 'In pulp science fiction,' according to Roberts, 'the most dangerous alien is the female alien who can mesmerise men through sexual allure or reproduce and overwhelm humankind'.[24] Within the fictional worlds of these texts, however, sex is beside the point, motherhood is vexed or not an issue, yet female agency is secure.

What remains open-ended in *Alien: Resurrection* is the meaning of Ripley's escape to earth. Certainly, there is intriguing irony (and grist for the movie mill) in the fact that the alien entity has indeed arrived, in the person of the woman who gave her life to prevent that from happening, and in the company of an android whose mission is to protect human life. Nevertheless, the emphasis in the closing scene of the film is on the bond between Ripley and Call, their mutual satisfaction, relief and comfortable companionship. In the closing lines of dialogue, Call, commenting on the beauty of earth, asks: 'What happens now?' Ripley responds, 'I don't know. I'm a stranger here myself.' Ripley's ambiguous last sentence reminds us that she is strange – not human – and therefore a threat. But more importantly, it reminds us of the parallels between the two female figures: both unnatural, both constructed, both alone in the sense of being without family, cohort, race, culture, species, without any of the ways of belonging that comfort us and make us peers. Each of them is in this respect precisely parallel to Frankenstein's monster, ripe for the kind of melancholy and despair that leads him to curse his maker and finally to immolate himself. Yet, the mood conveyed in the scene is one of curiosity and expectation rather than exhaustion, regret or retrospection.

Similarly, the bond emphasised in the preface introducing *Lives of the Monster Dogs* and the epilogue with which it ends is the friendship of adult females – the human Cleo Pira and the monster dog Lydia Petze. In her preface, Cleo writes: 'I'd like to thank Lydia Petze, who was also Ludwig's friend, for her help, and most of all for the sustaining friendship she's extended to me and, more recently, to my husband, Jim Holbrook, and our daughter, Eleanor, the first child in the world (I proudly believe) to be blessed with having a Samoyed for a godmother.'[25] Lydia, certainly the last of her line, raised in the company of others like herself, might have felt herself a lonely freak; instead she has moved forward, able to offer and to accept 'sustaining friendship'.

At the conclusion of these narratives, two females, peers, save one another from what Jonathan Crewe has termed 'apocalyptic melancholia'.[26] In spite of their singularity and the losses they have suffered, these female others are able to face the future because they have formed a bond with another female. Thus, in their intertextual dialogue with *Frankenstein*, *Lives of the Monster Dogs* and *Alien: Resurrection* are demonstrated two important ideological shifts: a refusal to accept radical loneliness as a rationale for apocalyptic despair, and a refusal to position women as mere victims or as powerful only by virtue of their sexuality and their control of reproduction. Moreover, these ideologies are vested in a different kind of alien: an alien who is and is not other. The valorisation of hybridity, of cyborg nature, in these works reflects and reinforces a significant current in postmodern thinking.

Notes

1. Mary Shelley, *Frankenstein*, ed. Johanna M. Smith (Boston: St Martin's Press, 1992), p. 101.
2. Peter Brook, *Body Work: Objects of Desire in Modern Narrative* (Cambridge, MA: Harvard University Press, 1993), p. 202.
3. Donna Haraway, *Simians, Cyborgs, and Women: The Reinvention of Nature* (New York: Routledge, 1991), p. 180.
4. Kirsten Bakis, *Lives of the Monster Dogs* (New York: Farrar Straus Giroux, 1997), p. 111.
5. Ibid., p. 225.
6. Ibid., p. 138.
7 Ibid., p. 71.
8. Ibid., p. 252.
9. Theodore Ziolkowski, 'Talking Dogs: The Caninization of Literature' in *Varieties of Literary Thematics* (Princeton, NJ: Princeton University Press, 1983), pp. 86–122. Ziolkowski traces the motif of the talking dog from Lucian's *Dialogues of the Dead*, fl.AD 160 through such

mid-twentieth-century works as Bulgakov's *The Heart of a Dog* (1928, published 1968).

10. Bakis, *Lives of the Monster Dogs*, p. x.
11. *Alien* (Ridley Scott, 1979); *Aliens* (James Cameron, 1986); *Alien3* (David Fincher, 1992); *Alien: Resurrection* (Jean-Pierre Jeunet, 1997).
12. Haraway, *Simians, Cyborgs, and Women*, p. 178.
13. Perlman played Vincent, the noble man/beast in the American TV series *Beauty and the Beast* from 1987–90, as well as the Sayer of the Law in John Frankenheimer's film of *The Island of Dr Moreau* (1996).
14. Bakis, *Lives of the Monster Dogs*, pp. 11–12.
15. Ibid., p. 30.
16. Ibid., pp. 4–5.
17. Ibid., p. 5.
18. Ellen Moers, 'The Female Gothic' in *Literary Women* (New York: Doubleday, 1974); reprinted in George Levine and U.C. Knoepflmacher (eds), *The Endurance of* Frankenstein: *Essays on Mary Shelley's Novel* (Berkeley: University of California Press, 1979), p. 81.
19. Moers, 'Female Gothic', p. 85.
20. Robin Roberts, *A New Species: Gender and Science in Science Fiction* (Chicago: University of Illinois Press, 1993), p. 40.
21. Shelley, *Frankenstein*, p. 140.
22. Roberts, *New Species*, p. 46.
23. Bakis, *Lives of the Monster Dogs*, p. 163.
24. Roberts, *New Species*, p. 41.
25. Bakis, *Lives of the Monster Dogs*, p. x.
26. Jonathan Crewe, 'Transcoding the World: Haraway's Postmodernism', *Signs*, 22: 4 (Summer 1997), p. 905.

Index